SHOT BY BOTH SIDES

WHAT WE HAVE HERE IS A FAILURE TO COMMUNICATE

EAON PRITCHARD

First published 2020

ArtScienceTechnology

artsciencetechnology.com

Maxine, Anthony and Hamish

CONTENTS

LES REMERCIEMENTS

Marcus Brown, Bill Drummond, Mark Earls.

Also, big thx to Wiemer Snijders, Kate Richardson,
Don Marti, Rob Schwartz, Rob Campbell,
Dave Trott, Giles/Sophie & the *Gasp!* posse,
Mark Pollard and Adam Pierno.
And everyone who bought or supported
the last book,
Cheers.

I wormed my way into the heart of the crowd,
I was shocked to find, what was allowed...

Howard Devoto/Magazine Shot By Both Sides 1978

OK, BOOMER.

Hello.

You're holding Eaon Pritchard's second book in your hands. It's excellent.

I have no idea who you are, why you're holding it, why you bought it, or how you got hold of your copy, but here we are - you with Eaon's book and me writing the foreword.

Maybe you're one of those eager middle managers who like to read a book over the weekend in the hope that you'll be a better manager on Monday. That never works, but here we are, you with Eaon's book and me writing its foreword.

You could, of course, be a junior advertising person looking to uncover the secrets of the communications industry. You're looking for the competitive advantage, that extra mile and the hidden insight that might get your idea into the pitch deck and in front of that fantastic top-of-mind high street brand.

It won't because that's not what this book is about, but here we are, you've bought the fucking book, and I'm still writing the bloody foreword.

Shot By Both Sides isn't a book about advertising. It isn't a book about management, strategic thinking or *hustlepreneurship* either.

It's a book about connections and a book for people who are interested in finding out how to discover them.

It's a book about two worlds: the art world and the wacky world of business communications: each with their impenetrable languages, pretensions, flamboyancies, angst and unbearably pretentious wankers.

Shot By Both Sides imagines each of these worlds having a sensible conversation with each other in the hope that they may find peace, or at least answers to their own particular lunacies. They won't, of course, but fuck it, it was worth a try.

Eaon Pritchard is the advertising industry's Bill Hicks. I know Eaon. I love him. I love him because he takes a grubby Scottish Generation X shaped finger and sticks it in the gaping wound of contemporary business while bellowing 'by the way, if anyone here is in advertising or marketing... kill yourself'.

What he's written here isn't a mirror, it isn't an exit either: this book, his book, is a survival handbook for the jaded of heart, or young whipper-snappers who smell a business rat, or the winners of pub quizzes or anyone who may have lost their way somewhere between art school and WPP.

This may not be the book you were looking for then, but here we are: this is the book Eaon has written.

No, this may not be the book you were looking for but it is the book you need.

And it's brilliant.

OK, Boomer - let's go.

Marcus John Henry Brown
Munich. January 2020

VOUS M'AVEZ MAL COMPRIS,
VOUS ÊTES IDIOT.

WILLEM, IT WAS REALLY NOTHING.

The rain falls hard on a humdrum town,
This town has dragged you down...

THE SS SHELLEY, A BRITISH FREIGHT ship ultimately bound for Argentina, finally reached the harbour in Newport News, Virginia in July 1926. Among its cargo were two young stowaways. Willem De Kooning, a 22-year-old house painter from Rotterdam, and his friend Leo Cohan. They had spent the voyage holed up, undetected in the ship's engine room.

Upon arrival in America, the two young men managed to *blag* their way into jobs as engine stokers on a ship to Boston from where they jumped a train to Rhode Island and snuck into Manhattan, avoiding immigration control at Ellis Island.

De Kooning had graduated from Rotterdam's prestigious Academy of Fine Arts the previous year. As an aside, the school was re-named after its most famous alumni in 1998, becoming the *Willem De Kooning Academie*, and alongside the possession of estimable fine art creds, the Academy is now widely regarded as the top school in the Netherlands for advertising and copywriting.

Students at the *Academie* of the '20s were immersed in *De Stijl*, the dominant Dutch art and architecture movement of the time. *De Stijl,* literally *The Style*, is instantly recognisable by simplified visual compositions of vertical and horizontal lines, using black, white and primary colours.

Whether Rotterdam is indeed a humdrum town I can't say, having never been, but young Willem, just like many other young European aesthetes before and since, had developed a fascination with all things Americana.

New York City really has it all, oh yeah.

In truth, Willem had bought into a relatively straightforward version of the American Dream.

The 1920s, after all, was the decade of prosperity, a new standard of living. Rising wages generated more disposable income for the purchase of consumer goods - Henry Ford had made car ownership a reality for many Americans. And advertising became as big an industry as the manufactured goods that advertisers represented.

Young Willem was determined to make it to New York, ditch his overalls and put his studies to use as a commercial artist.

If he could make it there, he'd make it anywhere.

(Some decades later this author, as a young art student in Scotland, was also drawn to the mythology of New York via the Ramones and CBGBs, Lou Reed and, of course, the young artists of the *Times Square Show* era of the early '80s.)

Willem made it. I didn't.

In a bit of strategic post-hoc myth-making, he changed his story for the art press many years later, claiming that it was the poetry of Walt Whitman and Frank Lloyd Wright's architecture that had captivated his imagination.

It could be argued that, given that one of the young De Kooning's principal interests was getting *beschonken*, there may have been other migratory choices more optimal than the prohibition-era USA.

Indeed, in the aftermath of World War 1 many prominent American writers and artists like Gertrude Stein, Ernest Hemingway, F. Scott Fitzgerald, T.S. Eliot and Ezra Pound had pissed off to ultra-bohemian Paris, where it was much easier to get a drink.

But it would be fair to say that New York City never truly accepted prohibition, and the 20's era kicked off the *new* New York – the New York of art, jazz, booze, narcotics, gangs, commerce, and culture. The city that doesn't sleep.

Willem's little town blues were melting away. In the Village, he initially found work as a sign-painter and window dresser. Still, it was in a low-rent studio space on Tenth Street that he discovered another kind of painting. He soon began to develop the *gonzo-exhibitionistic, romantic* chops that would eventually form his own distinctive take on the 'abstract expressionist' style. At the same time, honing a soon-to-be-legendary (and frankly world-class) drinking capability in the Village bars.

Soon the boozy *bohémien* had cemented his place among the group subsequently known as the 'New York School' that included - fellow Cedar Bar *pissheads* - Jackson Pollock, Robert Motherwell and Mark Rothko.

This scene is often portrayed as a *machismo* boys' club; however, that was not strictly true. Several women artists were Cedar bar regulars and fully paid-up members of the abstract expressionist 'club'.

Elaine de Kooning is perhaps the most well-known, she was also married to Willem. And Mary Abbott – who had studied under Barnett Newman.

Perle Fine and Helen Frankenthaler were also essential figures on the scene. Frankenthaler had developed her own unique 'staining' technique that later became the formula for 'colour field' painting.

Club membership was far more about drinking ability than gender.

It was this loose (in every sense) 'movement'

that was to eventually steal the spotlight from Paris as the new *avant-garde*, switch the poison of choice from absinth to bourbon and permanently shift the art world's attention to New York.

In some respects, De Kooning kept a strategic distance between himself and the other New York abstract painters by maintaining his figurative interest. Most memorably in his *Woman* series of paintings, beginning with *Woman I* in 1950.

By this time the abstract expressionist artists (and critics) had pretty much declared the human figure to be an *obsolete subject*. As de Kooning himself was enjoying king-of-the-hill status for the abstract compositions he had been producing over the previous years, this was something of a sidestep.

While some of his more purist peers saw *Woman I* as a kind of betrayal, a *regression back to an outmoded tradition*, WDK countered with the retort '*flesh is the reason oil paint was invented*'.

The influential art critic Clement Greenberg - best known for his early and enthusiastic championing of this abstract expressionism - soon became a big supporter of de Kooning's new figuration.

For Greenberg, de Kooning was 'the most advanced in our time' because of his unique ability to invest modern abstract art with the 'power of sculptural contour' from the human form. This located the artist's *Woman* paintings within a 'great tradition of sculptural draftsmanship' as exemplified by the likes of Leonardo, Michelangelo, Raphael, Ingres and Picasso.

This was De Kooning at the peak of his powers.

We hate it when our friends
become successful
And if they're noordelijk,
that makes it even worse.
And if we can destroy them,
you bet your life we will.

When he moved to up New York around 1950, southern boy Robert Rauschenberg was given short shrift from most of the hard-drinking abstract expressionists who hung out at the bars of the East Village. Jackson Pollock in particular.

He had studied under the guidance of Bauhaus luminary Josef Albers in North Carolina. Albers had tried in vain to give the lad some chops, but lack of talent was not going to hold back the fast-talking Robert, always at the ready with some loquacious Dada-esque quip.

Rauschenberg had already gained some nascent notoriety by 1951, producing a series of all-white paintings later shown at the fashionable Stable Gallery.

These 'White Paintings' were essentially blank canvases stretched in units of various sizes and combinations covered in everyday house paint applied with a roller.

But a background theory is essential, and Rauschenberg preferred to think of them as 'clocks'. *If one were sensitive enough that one could read it, that one would know how many people were in the room, what time it was, and what the weather was like outside.*

The avant-garde composer John Cage wrote a statement to accompany them.

'To whom: no subject, no image, no taste, no

object, no beauty, no message, no talent, no technique, no why, no idea, no intention, no art, no object, no feeling, no black, no white, no and.'

Nothing.

Cage later created his infamous *4' 33"* composition as a companion work.

4' 33" is a piece for full orchestra that comprises of the musicians not playing anything for precisely four minutes and thirty-three seconds.

Phew! Rock'n'roll.

Such was Rauschenberg's early versatility he followed up this collection with a series of 'Black Paintings' later that year.

Suspicious of all this self-conscious, quasi-intellectual, shallowness, the old guard never acknowledged him as a peer, and this irritated Bob.

'You have to have the time to feel sorry for yourself to be a good Abstract Expressionist,' he is said to have muttered.

But he had a plan. One evening in 1953 Rauschenberg found himself stood on the doorstep of Willem de Kooning's house in the East Village, his sweaty hands clutching a bottle of Jack Daniels.

The 27-year-old artist knocked hesitantly on the old master's door.

Don't be home, don't be home, he whispered shrinkingly to himself.

'But he was home,' Rauschenberg later recounted, 'And after a few awkward moments, I told him what I had in mind.'

MODERN LIFE IS RUBBISH

Drink to me, drink to my health,
You know I can't drink anymore.

SOME HISTORIANS WILL DATE the birth of modernism to around the late 17th century and the Scientific Revolution - closely associated with the Enlightenment. In many respects, the two overlap. Scientific thinking played a crucial role in the Enlightenment, as thinkers employed the scientific method to understand the world around them.

But modernism as *we* know it gets officially underway as a philosophical movement responding to cultural trends and changes arising from far-reaching transformations in Western society during the late 19th and early 20th centuries.

This was an era defined by the shock of industrialisation, the resulting massive urbanisation, rapid social change and advances in science. Not to mention new ideas in psychology, philosophy, and political theory.

This was a proper disruption.

What we tend to think of as *modernism* in the arts explicitly, spans a wide variety of artists and types of art. In painting, modernism would seem to begin properly with artists like Van Gogh and Cezanne in the late 19th century and then prevailed all the way through to the neo-expressionist work of another generation of New York artists like Schnabel and Basquiat in the 1980s.

The curious thing about the modernist transformation of painting - as compared with other art forms such as music or literature - is the speed with which it took off and how radical the change was.

Most art historians agree that Picasso's Les Demoiselles D'Avignon was the pivotal moment. Completed in 1907, although not publicly exhibited until 1916, 'Les Demoiselles...' was so outrageous that it is said to have upset even Picasso's absinthe-guzzling avant-garde buddies like Matisse and

Braque.

Later described as an *anti-idealist representation of unideal subject* – a distorted arrangement of Barcelona street prostitutes in African style masks - not only did *Les Des* subvert the illusion of three-dimensional perspective in favour of flat surface; but it also did away with pretty much all the other norms of representation visible in the previous 500 years of painting. It kicked off the cultural twentieth century, proper.

Picasso called it his 'first exorcism picture'.
L'Anarchie pour le Montmartre.

Despite the wide variety of painting over this time, the values driving the work are pretty constant—an emphasis on the importance of skill, originality and the personal expression of the individual artist.

And then somewhere around the mid-20th-century values began to change and a new thought— heavily influenced by the emergence of *postmodern philosophy*—begins to pull away from the modern focus on originality. This new work is initially distinct for its impersonal quality, often employing mechanical or *automated* techniques or even negating *skill* altogether.

The new *post*modern aesthetic rejected the master narrative of modernism wholesale and dismissed *the authority of high art* which modernism retained from the past. And so the previously essential qualities of individualism and originality, even notions of creativity itself, are targets for its *intellectual indignation*. For the most part, postmodern visual art appears easily repeatable, shallow art of the surface. Quotation, parody and irony preponderate this thinking because it arises from a deep-seated self-consciousness about the *theory of art*.

It was not the object itself that mattered.
But the conceptual processes behind it.

The first big star of the next generation was, of course, Andy Warhol. His use of silkscreen - removing the artist's direct touch - and subject matter derived from consumer goods, celebrities and mass production is perhaps the most famous example of the new wave counter to abstract expressionism.

In many respects, Warhol is the bridge from the modern to the *post*modern.

It was not unusual to play with pop forms before Andy, but they could be challenging to follow. Whereas Warhol's images of mass-produced objects are more immediately *gettable*. Either way, his individuality was still all over the work. And his 1970s return to painting—following a brief and chiefly unsuccessful dalliance with film (flirting with the more minimalist fundamental *nothingness*) - introduced more *expressionism* than had been present in his 60's *oeuvre*.

At the beginning of the 60's (which, let's face it, was still basically an extension of the '50s - the 60s really didn't kick in until 62/63 with Beatlemania and swinging London) Warhol had become acquainted with one Henry Geldzahler, an up-and-coming curator at the Metropolitan Museum of Art.

Geldzahler was taking an active interest in some of the new artists emerging in New York. It was Henry who had encouraged Andy – at this time an advertising illustrator keen to go full-time as a 'proper' artist - to try and find his own original 'style', and introduced the artist to indie gallery owner (and frequent host of art parties) Muriel Latow. According to legend, Latlow had asked Andy: 'Now tell me, Andy, what do you love more than anything else?'

'I don't know,' Andy said. 'Money?'

Muriel replied. 'Why don't you paint money, then?'

Andy thought that was a splendid idea, and Latlow is said to have charged Andy 50 bucks for the consultancy. Later on that evening she also suggested that Warhol also paint things that were *so familiar that nobody even noticed them anymore*. Like cans of Campbell's Soup. Warhol happily accepted this one too, although no cash changed hands for the bonus idea.

Incidentally, Warhol 'repaid' the initial favour to Geldzahler a few years later, making Henry the subject of a full length 'feature' film. Essentially 90-odd minutes of the subject smoking a cigar while becoming increasingly bored and irritated as the film progresses.

Warhol was now running in a variety of

directions with Latlow's advice and ordered up a large number of wooden boxes to be delivered to the Factory, his new studio on East 47th Street in midtown Manhattan. These boxes would shortly become the pieces in his first sculpture show.

Extending the soup cans idea, Warhol and his assistants screen printed the labels of other well-known consumer products on to the packages. Among the output of these sessions were the famous *Brillo Boxes*.

First exhibited at The Stable Gallery on West 58th street in 1964, more than any other early works it was these boxes that shot Warhol into superstardom, and prompt the Columbia University philosopher and critic, Arthur Danto to proclaim 'the end of western art!'.

What distinguishes a work of art from an identical-looking object that is not art?

This was the question posed by Danto in his influential 1964 article 'The Artworld' published in *The Journal of Philosophy*.

In *The Artworld* Danto breaks down art history into a succession of stages. The Mimetic stage, at which art *imitated* nature, was replaced by a *struggle of different styles* until the mid-nineteenth century until landing in the contemporary *post-historical stage* (*the end of art history*), as pioneered by the impressionists.

Danto's principal argument is that in the contemporary situation, it is now only the 'community' of art professionals (galleries, artists, critics – The Artworld) that can distinguish between what-is-art and what isn't.

Aesthetics has become a *completely autonomous area of knowledge.*

To Danto, the class of 64 – the Pop Artists, and the blurring of distinctions between 'high' art and mass culture - were *ambassadors of a new aesthetic reality.* A reality that could be only be understood only by other artists, academics, critics, and curators inhabiting *the Artworld*.

Andy's Brillo Boxes were at the centre of this thesis.

Warhol presided over a unique conveyor belt system that consciously blurred lines between the artist's individual authorship and mechanical reproduction.

This was a long way from DeKooning and the 'great tradition of sculptural draftsmanship' or indeed any of the abstract expressionist painting that had dominated the New York art scene just a few years earlier.

Warhol's boxes were ideologically closer to the work of French-American conceptual artist Marcel Duchamp, who's 'readymade' works from the turn of the century – some example pieces include a bicycle wheel, and a snow-shovel – predated Warhol by decades and presented mass-produced everyday objects, taken out of their usual context and promoted to the status of 'art' by the mere selection of the 'artist'.

Rather than mere enjoyment, or even just to be impressed by the technical skills of the artist, Duchamp wants to test our *intellectual responses* or tolerance level concerning what kinds of works a gallery can bring to the attention of its public.

(Duchamp's precise political leanings were ambiguous. Was he an anarchist or a Marxist? He was certainly adept at some decent Groucho

Marx-esque one-liners like '...*I contradict myself in order to avoid conforming to my own taste.*')

In a nutshell, Danto emphatically states that it is not possible to understand conceptual art without the sanctioning by the 'Artworld' and for an object to become art, the most important thing is that it must be appropriately *contextualised*.

This means its status depends totally on the context of the presentation and, naturally, a background theory.

The theory need not necessarily make any sense, of course.

ÇA PLANE POUR MOI

Scratched, ruined, exhausted, fulfilled,
You are the King of the couch!

MICHEL FOUCAULT IS BEST KNOWN as a philosopher, although he was a principally a historian. Most of his famous 60's *oeuvre* was *discourse analysis*, focusing on power relationships in society as expressed through language and practices. In particular, he studied how this played out as France shifted from a monarchy to democracy during the revolution of the 1790s.

Foucault wasn't all that interested in art. However, he did write a short book on Magritte and an essay on Velasquez formed the intro to his 1966 book *The Order Of Things*, a philosophical discussion of order - particularly the order of society - and the way that power operates in modern societies.

According to Foucault, knowledge and power are inseparable. He coined the term *power/knowledge* to illustrate this. Every exercise of power depends on the knowledge that supports it. Therefore, any claim to knowledge has the potential to advance the interests and power of certain groups while marginalising others.

For instance, even though the new forms of government no longer rely on torture, and public hangings as punishments, it still seeks to control people's bodies — by focusing on their minds.

In later works, particularly *Discipline and Punish* from 1975, Foucault argued that French society had reconfigured punishment. Rather than torture or public hangings it was the new practices of discipline and surveillance in institutions such as prisons, schools, and factories that produced compliant citizens.

We are coerced to act as though we are being watched. He would have had some fun commenting on the surveillance economy of 2019. We may have had fun reading it, although Foucault notoriously wrote prose so dense as to be almost impenetrable.

The linguist Noam Chomsky once noted that the ever-*erudite* Foucault– often cited as the most eminent of the poststructuralist and postmodernist thinkers, although, to his credit, he didn't like these labels - was actually intelligible if you sat him down and had a normal conversation.

(Unlike many of the other French philosophers).

Chomsky explains, 'I don't particularly blame Foucault for [obscurantism], it's such a deeply rooted part of the corrupt intellectual culture of Paris that he fell into it pretty naturally, though, to his credit, he distanced himself from it.'

Interestingly, Foucault confessed to his friend the American philosopher John Searle, that he intentionally complicated his writings to appease his French audience.

Searle has revealed that Foucault privately admitted, 'In France, you must make 25 per cent incomprehensible; otherwise people won't think it's deep–they won't think you're a profound thinker.'

The French structuralist Pierre Bourdieu claimed it was markedly worse than that. The BS quotient in the 'works' of Jacques Derrida, for example, is probably closer to 100%.

Derrida, another post-structuralist 'philosopher', *enfant terrible* of the French intelligentsia and *le vilain* responsible for developing the technique of semiotic analysis known as *deconstruction*, was so incomprehensible he made Foucault's texts read like Thomas The Tank Engine.

Foucault concurred, suggesting that Derrida practiced the method of *obscurantisme terroriste* (terrorism of obscurantism).

'He writes so obscurely you can't tell what he's saying, that's the obscurantism part, and then when you criticize him, he can always say, 'You didn't understand me; you're an idiot.' That's the terrorism part.'

I know what you're thinking.

'This is all very entertaining fella, but so far it's got Foucault to do with advertising.'

Well, *discourse is not the majestically unfolding manifestation of a thinking, knowing, speaking subject, but, on the contrary, a totality, in which the dispersion of the subject and his discontinuity with himself may be determined.*

Right?

In an amusing coincidence, the original commercial Brillo packaging *recontextualised* by Warhol was designed by a chap called James Harvey. A lower league abstract expressionist painter – *so far down he wasn't even on the map* - struggling to pay the bills through his art alone, he had bitten the bullet and taken a job in advertising!

Plus ça change, plus c'est la même chose, and advertising is still a business that few people aspire to join, in particular many among us who would much rather be directing movies, writing their novel or engaging in some form of 'activism' with their clients marketing budget rather than the grubby notion of getting people to buy car insurance or tile grout.

And so, closing the loop, the striking Brillo logo was designed by an action painter, a practitioner of precisely the kind of non-representational, raw expression art that Warhol was a reaction against.

Harvey wasn't a fan of Warhol's work, although he did attend the opening of the 1964 exhibition and is said to have had a long chat with Andy, but didn't mention having designed the original Brillo packaging. Never cross the streams.

'Making money is art, and working is art,
And good business is the best art.'

'*66 Scener Fra Amerika'* (66 Scenes from America) is a 1982 documentary film by Danish director Jørgen Leth.

It presents a variety of short vignettes with no discernible connecting narrative, other than exhibiting a seemingly random patchwork of objects and scenes that all together resembles a collection of cinematic postcards from a road trip. Essentially an experimental visual time-capsule of nothing-much-happening smack in the middle of life in Reagan-era America.

The film's best-known scene is a four and a half minutes long segment of Andy Warhol tucking into a Whopper from Burger King. An obvious pastiche of Warhol's signature film style, although the entire film is Warhol-esque.

While doing their research in advance of preparing a campaign for Burger King, the fast-food giant's agency stumbled upon the Andy footage on YouTube and took it to their client.

After much high-fiving and a year of wrangling with the various parties and rights owners, they had secured usage rights and set about preparing it to run as a showpiece in the advertising event of the year, the 2019 SuperBowl.

If not the most flamboyant, it is undoubtedly one of the more extraordinary SuperBowl ads of recent times when looked at from a philosophy of advertising standpoint. Not least in the way it spectacularly snatched defeat from the jaws of victory, as we shall see.

The Warhol/Burger King spot is, in effect, a 'readymade'.

Readymade was the term coined by Marcel Duchamp, exemplified by the notorious 1917 'sculpture', *Fountain*, which we will visit later.

Duchamp was initially a painter then turned sculptor. While he made his name as a *kinda* Cubist, he is widely regarded as one of the primary influencers in the rise of conceptual art. His *Nude Descending a Staircase, No.2* brought the house down at the 1913 New York Armory Show – even the Manhattan art public was scandalised by this European *weirdness* - however following that he pretty much abandoned painting and focused on 'sculpture', creating the first of his *'readymades'* in 1913.

The theory behind the readymade practice took a while to develop. It was finally explained in the editorial of the May 1917 issue of the avant-garde magazine *The Blind Man*, edited by Duchamp.

Whether Mr Mutt, with his own hands, made the fountain or not has no importance. He CHOSE it. He took an ordinary article of life, and placed it so that its useful significance disappeared under the new title and point of view – created a new thought for that object.

The object has been recontextualised.

There are three essential components to the readymade provision.

Number one; the choice of object is itself a creative act.

Number two; by doing away with the function of an object, it becomes art.

Number three; presenting the object as art gives it a new meaning.

In a nutshell, what is art is whatever the artist says is art.

This mini-manifesto represents the beginning of the movement towards conceptual art – and a post-modernism - as the status and relationship of the artist and the object are *called into question.*

The new postmodern artists disparaged modernists and their naive belief that a work of art could somehow appeal to a broad audience who had neither the time nor inclination to get up to speed with the latest continental philosophy gobbledygook.

Vous m'avez mal compris, vous êtes idiot.

If the readymade concept can be understood, at the very least, as a deliberate assault on the conventional understanding of the status and nature of art, is Burger King's use of an existing non-advertising object 'found' by the agency and recontextualised as a 45 seconds SuperBowl spot, an assault on the conventional understanding of the status and nature of advertising?

Almost. It is achingly close to being a *dialetheia*. Or a 'true contradiction'.

Had they pulled it off we could have been saying this Warhol film – this object - is an ad only insofar as it is not an ad.

It is what it is not, and this is why it is what it is.

This idea slightly offends objectivism, in where contradictions cannot be true – check your premises! - yet Burger King's spot is oh-so-close to being an ad that isn't an ad and a found object that is not just a found object.

YET IT IS ALSO BOTH.

Take the statement 'this sentence is false'.

This is the famous 'Liar's Paradox', the statement that everything being said is a lie. So, if the liar is lying, then the liar is telling the truth, which means the liar just lied, which means they're also telling the truth, which means it's a lie and so on, and so on.

With *Fountain* and many of his other 'sculptures', Duchamp's only contribution was to sign the object and exhibit it as art. Similarly, Warhol's only contribution to many of the works produced in his 'Factory' (including the Brillo Boxes) was to 'sign' or 'authenticate' them as art.

What are potentially true contradictions in media? Or advertising?

What is media insofar as it is not media?

What could we simply label as advertising by 'signing' it?

Burger King's marketing people were quoted in the press as saying 'we didn't want to change or touch the film in any way that would take away from its original intent'.

Yet they snatched defeat from the jaws of victory by adding the superfluous #eatlikeandy hashtag on the end frame.

Before the big game, BK's social media followers had been encouraged to claim a free Mystery Box Deal via UberEats style meal delivery service DoorDash. The box contained a silver wig, a bottle of ketchup and a Whopper voucher redeemable on game day. It was anticipated that recipients would don the wigs, eat the burger and post pictures and videos of themselves. And some of them did.

But now that made it an AD.

It then ceased to be what it is not – and became only what it is.

To simply run the film and sign it with the logo would have been it.

To allow simply the choice of object is itself to be the creative act.

What could be more of an all-American trilogy!

Andy, Burger King and the SuperBowl.

And a burger chain *decontextualizing and commodifying* an artist who famously adored advertising for its powers of *decontextualization and commodification.*

The balls to do that!
But they blew it at the last second.

By the inclusion of a *self-conscious, self-contradictory* (in the wrong way, keep up) and *self-undermining element*, what should have been a piece of supremely confident branding on the biggest stage instead becomes more like an overly hesitant parody.

And even after the fact, the boffins of mediocrity at Kellogg School of Management *guffed* in their assessment 'It's also unclear how many viewers will recognize Andy Warhol, who died in 1987, which limits the appeal of the commercial.' Kellogg could not be more wrong. Warhol is very much an artist of our time.

Self-commodification is now ubiquitous.

The idea of the Facebook 'friend' is not only a *reified* commodity but is also now increasingly becoming the way we understand the nature of authentic friendship.

Instagram influencers are not influential through possessing any particular expertise or knowledge. One now becomes an influencer by merely *declaring* oneself an influencer (a readymade!) - and Warhol's 15 minutes of fame dictum is more accurate than ever in the social media era.

Parody is, of course, distinct from pastiche.

Compromise is often thought to be in play when ideas have things taken OUT, but sometimes the most dangerous compromises are the things you put IN.

It can be the difference between an ok SuperBowl spot and what was nearly THE greatest SuperBowl spot of all time.

OPPOSITION TO THE SPECTACLE CAN PRODUCE ONLY THE SPECTACLE OF OPPOSITION

And every gimmick hungry yob,
digging gold from rock 'n' roll,
grabs the mic to tell us
he'll die before he's sold...

THIS GENERATION'S WARHOL is often said to be the 'street' artist Banksy.

There's a distinction between street art and graffiti writing and made by those in the know. Street artists are mostly making works intended for a general audience, the *passer-by*. In contrast, graffiti writers are often more concerned with competing with other graffiti writers first and foremost; any broader reach is a bonus.

Although, Banksy had started out as a graffiti *writer* around Bristol at the tail end of the 1980s.

He'd been drawn to the nascent hip-hop scene, focused around *The Wild Bunch* – a loose *sound system* collective - that included Nellee Hooper (who later went on to produce Soul II Soul, Madonna and Bjork), members of the future Massive Attack and others.

Like many of his musical contemporaries, Banksy has undoubtedly made a dent on a general audience. In 2010 *Time* magazine chose him for their list of the worlds 100 most influential people, alongside the likes of Barack Obama, Oprah, Steve Jobs and Lady Gaga.

It's easy to see why many make the connection with Warhol; the work of both draws on images from mass culture, both artists are hugely popular in the broader populace outside of the *Artworld* bubble while still commanding top dollar at auction. A significant amount of both artists output broadly privileges 'mechanical' production techniques – Banksy's stencils and Warhol's silkscreen printing. But those superficial similarities are, more or less, where the resemblance ends.

Andy was relatively apolitical, although once admitting he was conflicted. He *should* vote Republican as he loved money, loved the business of art and hated paying taxes. But artists obviously *ought to be* Democrats.

Whereas the Banksy brand – and hence its popularity with the current generation of young media types - has been built on an unequivocally anti-consumerist stance.

Of course, egalitarian anti-capitalist Banksy products can be bought by working-class people too, in poster shops in any suburban shopping centre or high street.

Banksy, or *Banksy Inc,* may also be conflicted in its own way.

Warhol was the son of working-class Slovakian immigrant parents, his father was a coal miner, and the boy grew up in a modest suburb of industrial Pittsburgh. In contrast, Banksy, while his name and identity remain the subject of some speculation, is widely understood to be *straight-outta* Yate. A leafy village in the Cotswold Hills about 12 miles from Bristol.

Although, after gaining some initial recognition via the *Bristol underground* scene he quickly got on his toes down the M4 to London and hopped onto the Metropolitan line tube to the abundantly more *for-real*, Shoreditch.

Banksy's anonymity has also allowed him to engage in some strategic myth-building. It is claimed that he was expelled from school (the notoriously brutal environment of Bristol Cathedral Choir School) and is reputed to have later done (a small bowl) of porridge after being nicked for *tagging*.

To be fair, maintaining anonymity outside of the circle of their own arena is a reasonably sensible, and standard, modus operandi of illegal graffiti writers. The *author-persona* Banksy has consciously and strategically extended this into his 'street' and *Artworld* brand.

The light-fingered Banksy also appropriated Andy Warhol's famous 'in the future, everyone will be world-famous for 15 minutes' soundbite in his 2006 exhibition *Barely Legal*. Anticipating the relentless march of self-commodification via social media and the surveillance economy, a computer screen flashes; 'in the future, everybody will be anonymous for 15 minutes.'

If Banksy's roots in the Gloucestershire *ghettos* are sub-optimal to his necessary 'authenticity', then a bit of strategic anonymity helps to fend off any accusations of *class tourism* – blending into the underclass as some kind of *cultural experience.*

Smoke some fags and play some pool, pretend you never went to school.

He shouldn't worry. In the UK, at least, the audience for hip-hop has always been largely white and middle-class. It ain't where you're *from*, its where you're *at.*

Perhaps Banksy's most well-known work is *Balloon Girl*, or to use its full correct title *There Is Always Hope.*

A *trademark* stencil job featuring a small girl reaching towards a heart-shaped balloon, the work originally appeared on the wall outside a printing shop in Shoreditch in 2002, and reappeared in various guises in other locations and as limited edition prints ever since.

Is the girl losing the balloon? Or about to catch it? Does it represent a loss of innocence? Or the arrival of hope and love?

Either way, in 2017 a poll conducted amongst UK consumers by consumer electronics giant Samsung, listed *Balloon Girl* as the 'people's number one' favourite artwork.

The bestowing of this honour riled the snooty Guardian art critic Jonathan Jones, who famously spluttered:

'Imagine how future generations will mock us for sanctifying Banksy, the *Boaty McBoatface* of modern art... Instead of portraying a rich human being with mysterious emotions, [Banksy] gives us a one-dimensional icon whose pathos is instantly readable...This makes him a brilliant propagandist. He never allows room for ambiguity...He has invented the artistic equivalent of a tweet. You see it; you get it. Is that really all we want?'

It turns out *The Artworld* do. And some art punters are willing to cough up considerably. In October 2018, a 2006 framed copy of the artwork was auctioned at Sotheby's, eventually selling for

£1,042,000 – a record price for the artist.

Moments after the closing bid, to the horror of the attendant *Artworld* and the assembled press and TV news, the artwork began to self-destruct employing a hidden mechanical paper shredder that Banksy had built into the frame bottom.

The buyer was happy though, Banksy Inc authenticated the 'new' work and renamed it 'Love in The Bin'. Geddit?

Another one of the many Banksy commentary pieces on consumerism is '*Early man goes to market*'. This one is a bit more interesting, a 'rock painting' rather than stencil, portraying a primitive human pushing a shopping cart in the style of prehistoric cave painting.

'Early Man...' showed up mysteriously in the British Museum in 2007 – smuggled in by Banksy's people. The label claimed that the 'fossil' had been found in the Peckham district south of London and it remained on show for several days. None of the museum staff noticed the hoax exhibit.

(Archness notwithstanding, and from an evolutionary perspective, Banksy inadvertently

presents the link missing in much of today's consumer research. Because modern consumers still have the minds of our early ancestors and are directed by motives that were shaped a long time ago.)

In a final ironic twist, 'Early Man...' later returned to display in the same museum, this time at the institution's request, as part of an exhibit examining objects which 'challenge the official version of events and defy established narratives'.

Much of Banksy's style challenges concepts of originality and authenticity, albeit a tad opaquely. 'Early Man...' is among several fake *artefacts* he smuggled into the exhibitions of various museums around this time.

In 2005 alone, he *punked* the MOMA, the Metropolitan Museum of Art, the Brooklyn Museum, and the American Museum of Natural History in New York. All fake exhibits were carefully integrated, mimicking the exhibition style and signage of the museums.

In this way, the installations echoed Duchamp's declaration in *The Blind Man* - it is the presence of the object in the institution of the museum which has made it, de facto, authentic.

It was in 2015 that Banksy launched perhaps his most ambitious *spectacle* to date. '*Dismaland*' was an exhibition in the seaside resort town of Weston- super-Mare in Somerset, England that took the form of a dystopian theme park billed as 'the UK's most disappointing new visitor attraction'.

A *bemusement park*.

Built on what are now standard Banksy themes; apocalypse, anti-consumerism, and 'critiques' on celebrity culture, it featured artworks from over 50 artists including fellow activists Jenny Holzer and Caitlin Cherry, alongside Damian Hirst, Jimmy Cauty and ten Banksy artworks. Musical performances were provided by Pussy Riot and Banksy's old mates from Bristol, Massive Attack.

It should have been great, but Dismaland sadly lived up to its billing, a disappointment. Tedious and humourless, a one-dimensional *pseudo-event* in real life – but one that looks impressive reported in Vox.

One notable Banksy inclusion is 'The Big Wave'.

A tsunami is about to crush a working-class family on the beach. They can't see the wave – they are looking in the wrong direction surrounded by their array of consumer products, sun cream and the like. Aaargh.

VOUS ÊTES IDIOT.

Attendants around the park hold bunches of black balloons, which exhibit goers can take home, 'I am an imbecile', they proclaim.

But what is Banksy attacking?

The cultural imperialism of American corporations like Disney?

Or the cretinous working class for being passively complicit in the 'consumer society' and simply too stupid to see what's really going on?

The irony here is that he steps dangerously close to sharing this contempt for the idiocy of ordinary punters with his *Boaty McBoatface* critic, Jonathan Jones. *Oups!*

In reality, much of seaside Britain *is* Dismaland! But without the irony. Effectively ghost towns, many are more deprived and neglected than their more famous cousins, the inner-city.

Key attractions include severe poverty, unemployment, dumping grounds for the mentally ill, ex-con no-hopers and substance abusers. Never mind the dodgems here's the methadone clinic.

The heyday of Britain's seaside resorts is long gone. The factory worker *beano* to Blackpool or the family week at Butlins was all but over by the 70s as cheap air travel to Spain and the surrounding Med suddenly became available to working-class families.

Nobody went to the English seaside who could afford to go somewhere else.

Interestingly, Margate, the traditional seaside day out for East London and Essex dock workers, is the childhood home of artist Tracey Emin who shot to fame on the back of a nomination in the 1999 Turner Prize. Emin grew up in there in the 1970s, when the Kent resort was still attracting crowds of holidaymakers. Margate has now reinvented itself as the art capital of south-east England (Shoreditch-on-Sea) reopening its Dreamland proper amusement park and hosting the Turner

Contemporary, a museum inspired by the town's association with J. M. W. Turner and the venue for the 2019 Turner Prize.

Turner himself was featured high on the list of the top 20 all-time favourite artists in the UK. The poll, conducted by YouGov, features a range of artists including impressionists, sculptors, masters and painters from the 14th century right up to the modern-day. Turner snuck in at number six. Just behind Leonardo Da Vinci, Vincent Van Gogh, Constable, Monet and – at number one? – you guessed it.

Donald Trump famously said during the 2016 campaign that he could 'shoot somebody on 5th Avenue in New York, and he wouldn't lose any voters.' As each Banksy intervention appears to heap more contempt on us, the *brainwashed consumer morons*, the more we love him!

The final contradiction of Banksy is that one of the keenest critics of 21st-century consumer society is one of its *most media-savvy cultural entrepreneurs*. The artist-in-residence of the new elite.

Of course, there has always been a very lucrative market for art that takes a swipe at capitalism. And *anti-consumerist* consumerism.

The historian and political analyst Thomas Frank famously noted: 'Capitalism has amassed great sums by charging admission to the ritualised simulation of its own lynching.'

Banksy has never been shy about an intransigent antipathy towards advertising.

'The people who truly deface our neighbourhoods are the companies that scrawl giant slogans across buildings and buses trying to make us feel inadequate unless we buy their stuff.

'You owe the companies nothing. Less than nothing, you especially don't owe them any courtesy. They owe you. They have re-arranged the world to put themselves in front of you. They never asked for your permission, don't even start asking for theirs.'

That now-infamous tirade was penned back in 2004.

In 2019, slogans across buildings and buses are least of our worries. Advertisers re-arranging the world to put their message in front of us seems positively *polite* in comparison to *the unilateral claiming of private human experience as raw material for product development and market exchange by the surveillance economy.*

And so, by *occupying* the public space Banksy is adapting the 'language' of consumer brands to promote a critical reception of *images*—a mode of response that 'calls into question' their intended meanings. A kind of *détournement.*

A salient example is the Napalm girl stenciled with Mickey Mouse and Ronald McDonald either side of her.

But what exactly is being called into question, here?

Professor Byron Sharp and his colleagues at the Ehrenberg Bass Institute, the worlds centre for evidence-based marketing and marketing science, would pass Banksy with top marks.

He would have waltzed through Mark Ritson's brand management mini-MBA.

If anything, he is the exemplar of sophisticated mass marketing.

The key to growing a brand is to build 'market-based assets', and these come in two assortments – maximised distribution (physical and digital availability) – and clear and distinctive branding *cues* that are easy to notice and recall.

The real challenge of advertising is all about mental availability.

This means getting noticed in the first place - grabbing attention – and then using that attention to refresh and build memory structures, strengthening existing associations that make the brand easy to notice and easy to buy.

Even anti-establishment artists seem to have no qualms about the commercial distribution of their work on print, merchandise, and clothing.

They talk the talk, a discourse of resistance to advertising, while walking a different walk, using their art as a form of advertising.
But it's ironic, right?

It is this supposedly *reflexive and ironic* aspect

that separates Banksy's work from straightforward marketing strategies. Or does it?

A background theory is essential.

'I say something I don't actually mean, and expect you to understand not only what I actually do mean but also my attitude toward it.'

But is this too conceptual for consumers, who just want to *exit via the gift shop* with a little piece of anti-consumerism consumption to signal their disdain for consumption to other consumers?

In a way, this is Banksy's own *dialetheia*. Or a 'true contradiction'.

It is what it is not, and this is why it is what it is.

Is advertising any different? It contains its own reflexivity, or self-consciousness, each ad calls attention only to *its own status as a production.*

So, let's just pump the music up and count our money.

In *Subculture: The Meaning of Style* by sociologist Dick Hebdige - a structuralist examination of UK youth subcultures from the 50's to late 70's - the author outlines how argues that it is through style, and the subversion of everyday objects, that subcultures can separate themselves from the mainstream culture to which they belong. Besides, subcultures almost always stem from some sort of *deviance*, and also almost always emerged out of working-class culture.

Working-class youth can manage their *status problems* by creating a new *sub* or *counter*-culture and establish new norms that don't conform to those of the dominant culture's. The *new* models, or style, contain their own ideological meanings and symbolic forms of resistance.

Of course, subcultures often take objects and styles of the dominant mainstream culture and appropriate them to demonstrate a new meaning.

However, every *counter-culture* idea of any significance is sooner-or-later doomed to be incorporated or *co-opted* by the establishment.

Firstly, the mainstream media discovers the subculture and reacts with moral panic, exposure to the subculture then expands membership drawing in more participants while in the process losing any rebellious edge either by becoming commodified - another commercial consumer product - or by media *exoticising* its members, representing them as *harmless clowns*.

Once too many people get on the bandwagon, it forces the originals to get off.

Get your ACIEEED smiley face t-shirts with this coupon in your soaraway Sun!

What was 'otherness' is reduced to 'sameness'.

This incorporation minimises *otherness* and then ultimately defines the subculture in precisely the terms that it originally sought to resist in the first place.

What began as symbolic challenges end up becoming the new conventions.

The mainstream can play its own games of *détournement!*

The Sex Pistols classic punk-era Silver Jubilee anti-anthem 'God Save The Queen' was played *at* the Queen - as an enduring symbol of Britishness - at the opening ceremony of the London Olympics in 2012! In Journey Along the Thames, a two-minute film by *Trainspotting* director Danny Boyle the song plays as the camera ironically maps the same route the band took in the infamous boat trip on the Queen Elizabeth, between Tower Bridge and Westminster, in 1977.

On November 3rd 2016, Andrew Rosindell, a Conservative MP, argued for a return to the broadcasting of the national anthem (*God Save the Queen*) at the end of BBC broadcasting each day (this had dropped in 1997, mainly due to 24-hour broadcasting), to commemorate the outcome of the Brexit vote.

That night BBC Two's Newsnight programme obliged, ending its nightly broadcast with a clip of the Pistols' song.

But surely, if a subculture could somehow resist incorporation - and not 'sell-out' - it could prevail, with values intact?

But what if there is/was no subculture in the first place? What if mainstream culture and counter-culture were simply two sides of the same coin?

What if consumer capitalism was not about conformity at all, but actually depended upon rebellion and counter-culture absolutely, to generate the next wave of rebel product for integration into the mainstream?

This is the argument put forward by Heath and Potter in *The Rebel Sell - Why the Culture Can't Be Jammed*. That consumption is not about conformity at all - but distinction.

Cultural products that are purchased to display that we are smarter, cooler, more 'authentic' than others, generate competitive consumption.

Heath and Potter further argue that the cycle perpetuates itself because one the early adopters see too many people jumping on the latest counter-cultural bandwagon, they get off and move onto something else. *L'incohérence* being that anti-consumerist consumers are often the most brand conscious.

> *They can fool themselves into believing that they don't care because their preferences are primarily negative. They would never be caught dead driving a Chrysler or listening to Celine Dion. It is precisely by not buying these uncool items that they establish their social*

superiority.

(It is also why, when they do consume 'mass society' products, they must do so 'ironically'—to preserve their distinction.)

In an interview in The Observer, to promote his radio show on BBC6 Music, former Clash associate, Roxy club DJ, film director and Big Audio Dynamite musician, Don Letts bemoaned, 'These days, people get into music to be part of the establishment. The most f-you guy around is Justin Bieber. What does that mean? There's no counter culture – only over-the-counter culture.'

While Don laments the passing of youth culture rebellion, as some sort of force for the critique of mass society, it is this loss that represents more of a challenge to the future of consumer capitalism.

There is no longer any significant counter-culture from which to draw the next wave of cultural consumer products.

Selling out is now no longer something that needs to be post-rationalised to stave off cognitive dissonance in rebellious youth.

Selling-out *is* the objective, right from the get-go! For influencers in the west or 'Key Opinion Leaders' in the east. Although what they are influential *in*, or what these key opinions *are*, remains somewhat opaque.

For battle-scarred Gen Xers like your author, this is a hard one to swallow.

Not so for millennials, the previous generations' ideas of 'rebellion' have never been part of their culture.

(The real genius of Uber, for example, is nothing to do with technology or even the deft sidestepping of regulatory obstacles and corporation tax.

The genius of Uber is in turning a commodity (consumption) product – the Taxi – into a display (status) product and spinning its anti-unionisation, anti-regulation winner-takes-all form of ultra-capitalism as some sort of signal of non-conformity and rebellion.)

When did music, once at the centre of youth culture lose its importance?

Are we finally over the counter-culture?

1980 was the year that the generation labelled millennials began being born. Therefore, the early guard started to enter their teens around 1993 – and this is also the year that the internet starts to be adopted and began its ten-year march towards critical mass.

A year earlier in 1992, The KLF – the art-rave concept 'band' formed in 1987 by Bill Drummond and Jimmy Cauty, on a mission to destroy the mainstream music industry - were at the peak of their powers. They were scheduled to appear on the televised Brit Awards show, to perform and collect the award for 'Best Act'.

Theatre maverick and legend Ken Campbell had been Bill Drummond's mentor –and would later direct Bill and Jimmy's one-off 'Fuck the Millennium' performance at London's Barbican in 1997. He gave Drummond the following advice:

Don't bother doing anything unless it is heroic.

In one final act of heroic defiance, Drummond and Cauty took the stage backed up by Extreme Noise Terror (hardcore punk-death metal hybrid thrashers) and performed a barely recognisable *grindcore* (heavily distorted and sped up) rendition of their biggest hit *3 am Eternal* before Drummond sprayed the audience with (blank) bullets from a machine gun.

As the ensemble departed the stage, the PA announces:

'The KLF have left the music business.'

'In a strange way, something about the music industry did die around that point', says KLF biographer John Higgs.

Up until the early 90s, the history of the twentieth-century pop culture and style was all about *invention* and *innovation*. Completely new musical genres popping up roughly every ten years or so was the norm.

I like this little thought experiment. Consider *Heartbreak Hotel* from '56 and *Strawberry Fields Forever* from '66. Only ten years apart, but they feel like they are from different planets. Ten years after that was *Anarchy in the UK*, then another quantum leap to *What Time is Love?*

But lift just about any pop/rock/dance/R'n'B hit

from 2009 and drop it into 2019, it sounds like it could have been made yesterday.

The 20th-century pop continuum was something else. From jazz and blues into rock 'n' roll, then rhythm and blues, psychedelic rock, Motown and soul. The 70s ushered in prog rock, reggae, heavy metal, disco and punk, and the 80s unleashed hip-hop, techno and house and loads more.

Higgs notes 'The assumption was that this level of creativity was normal and would continue indefinitely.... It would never have occurred to anyone in those seats, as Drummond fired blanks into the ranks of their peers, that this period of invention had come to an end'.

As the last round emptied from Drummond's machine gun, the *last train to trancentral* lurches out of the station. Like the austere busses on the back of Jamie Reid's iconic *décollage* sleeve for the Sex Pistols 'Pretty Vacant' single from '77, pop music as *incendiary* in mass culture began its final graceless journey, towards its ultimate destination.

Nowhere and boredom.

Is it that the emergence of devices and services

that, at first look, appeared to democratise the music industry, shifting the power dynamic and giving us access to all music, all for free, was an incorporation or co-optation too far?

Or did music begin to lose its signalling and galvanising power because it became an individualised 'pleasure' commodity product consumed (for free) by individuals in private within their earbuds? Or just background noise to something else.

Either way, our relationship with music had now changed forever – seemingly overnight; therefore consumer capitalism's (profitable) relationship with the counter-culture has also begun to change.

Guess who's back, guess who's back?
Guess who's back, guess who's back?
Guess who's back, guess who's back?
Guess who's back?

Banksy thinks…. 'this looks like a job for me…'

Where art irritates life.

This was the strapline announcing the opening of the official Banksy store, *Gross Domestic*

Product, in South London in 2019, a line any advertising copywriter would have been proud of.

But GDP more than just a shop, it's promulgation on consumerism.

Where you can buy Banksy merch.

Ironically.

But with real money.

Among the products for sale include the Union Jack stab-proof vest as worn by grime superstar Stormzy on stage at the Glastonbury festival, and disco balls made from discarded police riot helmets.

In the past, Banksy has never manufactured, sold or offered for sale goods bearing his brand although unauthorised copying of Banksy works is pretty widespread.

Banksy Inc claims that they have been forced to release the branded merchandise to protect his trademarks - owners of registered trademarks are expected to use their brands in the course of trade properly.

At the end of 2018, Pest Control, the division

that authenticates Banksy artworks, took action against an Italian company that organised a Banksy exhibition in Milan's Mudec Museum.

The court in Milan sided with Pest Control, enforcing *the trademark*, and ordering the museum to stop selling 'branded' merchandise - notebooks, diaries, postcards, etc. - featuring images including the iconic mural *Flower Thrower,* a stencil piece depicting a protester lobbing a bunch of flowers instead of a petrol bomb.

Why would Banksy not simply copyright his artworks instead of registering trademarks?

Copyright is a much better mechanism for protecting artistic IP, whereas trademarks are designed to protect logos, taglines and other brand assets.

Sadly, Banksy has been a bit too vocal in his parroting of the 'copyright is for losers' party-line.

But are trademarks not equally unacceptable, on the same grounds?

Another explanation is more straightforward.

Starting a copyright legal action would require

Pest Control to show that it enforces the copyright on behalf of the artist.

But this would mean revealing Banksy's real identity, which runs the risk of damaging the riddle of the brand.

Where there's a mystery, there's a margin.

It is the eternal paradox of counter-cultural products. When they succeed, they must surely become embedded into the structures they were originally directed against.

Death or glory becomes just another story.

After all that, I'm available and happy to straighten out the brand strategy, Robin.

WILLEM IT WAS REALLY NOTHING (REPRISE)

I don't dream about anyone,
Except myself.

RAUSCHENBERG IS ON THE doorstep of Willem de Kooning's house in the East Village, clutching a bottle of Jack Daniels.

'I don't really trust ideas; especially good ones' is one of Robert's many trademark one-liners. This particular idea is a cracker.

In many respects, the foundation for what we now understand as conceptual art, comes in no small measure from Rauschenberg's rapid popularisation of the *Dada*-based position that the *artist has the authority to determine* the definition of art.

One salient example is his 1961 'portrait' of Iris

Clert, made for an exhibition at her eponymous gallery in Paris, which consisted of a telegram from Bob that stated: 'This is a portrait of Iris Clert if I say so/ Robert Rauschenberg.'

Willem lets Rauschenberg in, they have a couple of drinks from the bottle of Jack and Rauschenberg pops the question.

He asks De Kooning for a drawing.

Bob explains to Will that his intention is to completely erase the drawing and exhibit the resulting *conceptual* piece.

Rauschenberg wants to 'explore' whether an artwork could be produced entirely through *erasure*—an act focused on the removal of marks rather than their *accumulation*.

As they polish off the rest of the bottle, De Kooning reluctantly agreed - where's the harm, these cheeky young postmodernist scamps should be humoured, he supposed. However, the wily Willem didn't want to make Rauschenberg's destruction job too easy, so he asked Bob to come back in a couple of days. In the interim DK revisited the drawing, layering on an extra selection of different media and techniques - pastels, pencils, crayon, charcoal, and ink, anything to make the erasing as difficult as possible.

One of Rauschenberg's heroes was, naturally, Marcel Duchamp. Duchamp had famously exhibited his own *destruction* 'painting' in 1919—a cheap postcard reproduction of Leonardo's *Mona Lisa* with a cartoon moustache added. The name of the piece, *LHOOQ*, is a pun in French; the acronym sounds a bit like '*Elle a chaud au cul*', or '*She has a hot ass*'.

(If he hadn't been one of the key figures in the emergence of conceptual art, he could have had a start as a junior copywriter, although that kind of pun wouldn't go down well in an ad agency in 2019)

Let's take another look back at Duchamp's earlier 1917 'sculpture', *Fountain*.

Designed to *shift focus in art from physical craft to intellectual interpretation* [sic], *Fountain* was a standard urinal purchased from Fifth Avenue hardware store and submitted into the first exhibition of the Society of Independent Artists at The Grand Central Palace in New York.

Often described as 'the most influential modern work of art, ever', the original urinal was lost sometime in 1917 and is only known from one blurry photograph. To see it today, several 'replicas', authorised by Duchamp Inc, can be found all around the world, including the Centre Pompidou of Paris, the Tate Modern in London and the San Francisco MoMA.

The irony is that if you go to one of those galleries and you see one of these phoney 'replicas', it will be a unique piece. All 'fakes' have to be handcrafted individually by an artisan ceramic artist—the original mass-produced urinals have not been manufactured industrially since the '50s.

It is what it is not,
and this is why it is what it is.

(In another twist, it turns out that 'Fountain' may have actually been the 'work' of Dada artist and poet Baroness Elsa von Freytag-Loringhoven, a friend of Duchamp's who entered it on his behalf, distancing the 'artist' even more).

Either way, the philosopher and fierce critic of postmodernist gobbledygook, Stephen Hicks makes a valid point in his famous 2004 essay '*Why Art Became Ugly.*'

He asserts that Duchamp is making a deliberate statement, he didn't select just any ready-made object to display.

'*He could have selected a sink or a doorknob. In selecting the urinal, his message was clear: Art is something you piss on.*

Postmodernists, the worst of them anyway, are people of deep ressentiment (note: a word from French adopted by Nietzsche to describe an even more embittered extension of the English 'resentment'). *Bitterness, envy, and rage leads them to lashing out with an intent to destroy any aspect of culture that seems to be opposite.*'

Or only insanity that opens up the doors for a mountain of bullshit masquerading as art.

The 2019 Turner Prize debacle is a hilarious case in point. Amongst themselves, the four artists nominated decided there should be no single winner. The four have much in common, apparently – an interest in power and agency, exclusion and oppression.

The work ranged from a performance piece 'imagining a post-patriarchal world' to an installation created out of sound effects and distortions to evoke *aural memories* from survivors of the Saydnaya prison in Syria. And so on.

You get the picture.

(Of course, addressing an issue isn't the same as *addressing a public* and the big problem with so much of this clumsy overtly political 'art' favoured by the likes of The Turner Prize is that it basically lacks anything resembling an idea.)

'Let's write the phrase 'Middle Class' in large blocks of ice and leave the blocks to melt in parks outside the Republican and Democratic conventions, yeah?'

(American Democratic Presidential candidate Elizabeth Warren's 'Rebuild the Middle Class' campaign line was hilarious to us Brits, of course.

Yes! 24 Hour Waitrose! Pine nuts for all!)

Apparently, one artist froze a thousand little figurines and sat them on some Berlin city steps in the summer. They melted.

And we plebs are all taught a lesson about global warming, right?

In their joint statement, the *Turner Four* announced that pitting themselves against each other 'would undermine our individual artistic efforts to show a world entangled. The issues we each deal with are as inseparable as climate chaos is from capitalism.'

Perhaps awarding a single prize would have 'privileged' one marginalised faction over another.

That would never do?

(One finalist is reputed to have once flushed away his British passport in a plane toilet in a moment of rebellion against the 'privilege' it confers.)

'So, we will split the prize money equally, ten grand each.'

It took Rauschenberg nearly two months to almost completely erase the de Kooning original.

The result, a *triumph of emptiness*, was presented in a plain gilded frame with an inscription handwritten by Jasper Johns - 'Erased de Kooning Drawing, Robert Rauschenberg, 1953'.

In an ironic twist that would, no doubt, have amused Willem, the San Francisco MOMA - where the 'painting' now resides - subsequently used the latest digital processing technologies available in 2010 to reveal the original de Kooning drawing!

The museum stuck to the script in asserting that the power of *Erased de Kooning* remains, derived from *'the allure of the unseen and from the enigmatic nature of Rauschenberg's decision...'*

Was it an act of homage, provocation, humour, destruction, or, as Rauschenberg once suggested, a celebration?

Or the final mystery of mysteries?

Poetry, nothing
Music, nothing
Painting and dancing, nothing
The world's great books
A great set of nothing
Lots and lots and lots of nothing,
nothing, nothing, nothing, nothing, nothing.

Nothing.

THIS IS THE POSTMODERN WORLD

It's the dialectic paradigm of reality,
constructivist neo-cultural theory
and rationalism, baby.

LEGENDARY MARKETER SERGIO ZYMAN
served two stints at Coca-Cola, from 1979 to 1986
and then a second time from 1993 to 1998. His
watch oversaw some big successes, including iconic
campaigns 'Coke Is It!' and 'Always Coca-Cola.' He
also managed hugely successful Coke brand
extensions such as Diet Coke and Cherry Coke.

Despite those *hits* Zyman best-known for a
couple of *flops*. The first is the *New* Coke 'disaster'
from 1985.

New Coke was originally released as a
reformulation of Coca-Cola designed to combat
Pepsi in the 'taste test'. Pepsi had briefly stolen

share and challenged Coke's market dominance.

But within three months, the new product was dumped following consumer backlash, Coca-Cola Classic was back on the shelves, and Zyman had departed, staying away from *Coke Towers* for nearly ten years.

In the mid-90s Coke - still with one cautious eye on Pepsi - were searching new to appeal to the next generation, the *slackers*, the grunge kids who were thought to be 'immune' to conventional advertising language and rejectors of *shiny packaging and jingles.*

Zyman was back at the controls, and the resulting innovation was *OK Soda.*

The catalyst was a generational study originating out of MIT, that seemed to nail down how to reach the elusive Generation X.

'Economic prosperity is less available than it was for their parents, Even the traditional rites of passage, such as sex, are fraught with life-or-death consequences. [Nineteen-year-olds] are very accustomed to having been manipulated and knowing that they're manipulated'.

(Does any of this sound familiar? Perhaps you've read about how Millennials/GenZ/MillXZennials have turned the traditional marketing strategy on its head, requiring an entirely new approach blah blah blah...)

Coke's agency, Wieden+Kennedy, uncovered some further research that indicated *Coca-Cola* was the second most recognised phrase in the world, across all languages and cultures. The first was *OK*, which was coincidentally also the two middle letters of *Coke*. Who would pass up the opportunity to be numbers 1 AND 2?

And so OK Soda arrived, it would be positioned as the *anti*-Coke (but made by Coke).

Coke is a feeling, right? And so was OK Soda. But the Gen X feeling was one of *disillusionment with the products of 20th-century capitalism,* and the *movement* had its own Situationist-esque manifesto with some splendid one-liners.

What's the point of OK? Well, what's the point of anything?

OK Soda reveals the surprising truth about people and situations.

OK Soda may be the preferred drink of other people such as yourself.

(In 2019 when many brands can't even pull together one coherent line that even makes any sense - *Verb* your *adjective,* ughhh - OK Soda had dozens of them!)

The campaign featured some eerily prophetic interactive elements, including a phone-in hotline - 1-800-I-FEEL-OK. 'Your comments may be used in advertising or exploited in some other way we haven't figured out yet.'

Taking a 'situationist' leaf out of Malcolm McLaren's *Swindle* cookbook, the agency placed some of its own negative 'reviews' to create faux-backlash.

A sequence of TV commercials, in the oxymoronic form of a *chain-letter*, added to the surreal nature of the campaign.

'What does it mean to receive a chain letter in the context of a thirty-second spot? It's completely, utterly meaningless.'

The OK Soda campaign was the first to take the

Dadaist *anti-art* philosophy and apply it to a major brand as 'anti-advertising' on such a scale. And arguably set the blueprint for all manner of future interactive advertising once the technology had caught up with the ideas. (OK Soda's advertising was easily about ten years ahead of its time).

When it launched, Coke predicted that OK Soda would rake in a billion dollars and 4 per cent of the US market. But by 1995 it was off the shelves and DOA. The anti-advertising brand turned out to *be only advertising*. No-one bought it (yet...)

Irony may yet have its day, New Coke, supposedly one of the biggest marketing flops in American history, is returning to the shelves, on the back of product placement in 'Stranger Things', the Netflix teen-horror series set in...1985.

OK Soda didn't fly, but the influence is strong.

They nailed it, but couldn't scale it. However, in hindsight, OK Soda opened the door for a new wave of *postmodern* advertising.

It's difficult to explain postmodernism in any straightforward way.

Even in a very basic sense, we need to make at least one important distinction; that between postmodern *culture* and postmodernist *theory*.

Postmodern culture, or 'postmodernity', is the epoch in history in which we are living. This is the stuff that philosophers, media types and cultural anthropologists need to be interested in as they (some of them, anyway) try to make sense of the times.

Getting anyone to agree on a definition of postmodern culture is tough. For some, it represents the next *creative renaissance* for others, it's the end of the world.

Postmodern theory, or 'postmodernism' *proper*, refers to the group of philosophers and critics (mostly French and some of whom we've met earlier), affected by the postmodern culture, and who *call into question* the validity of modernist concepts like reason and science.

For example, Jean-François Lyotard argues that scientific research has lost its way. He claims it doesn't set out to uncover knowledge for a better understanding of the world, but only advances the power interests of those rich enough to fund it. Hence, we have a steady stream of bigger and better nuclear weapons but still no cure for cancer.

Many postmodern*ists* hold some sort of *grab bag* mix of the following views:

There is no objective reality; there is no scientific or historical truth, tools such as science, technology, reason and logic are not vehicles of human progress but *suspect instruments of established power*.

Moreover, postmodernists deny there is such thing as *human nature*. All aspects of human behaviour and human psychology are socially constructed, so no theory of the natural or social world can be correct as all are illegitimate *metanarratives*. Even language refers to nothing outside of itself.

If that's not confusing enough, postmodern*ism* also refers to aesthetic/cultural products and art, some of which – like Banksy *et al.* and OK Soda, to a degree – *critique* aspects of postmodernity as its subject, although that is not always necessary.

Now, you might think a prototypical postmodern *art* piece would be Carl Andre's Equivalent VIII, one of a series of 'sculptures' made in 1966. You know the one, the 'bricks'.

The Tate Gallery in London quietly acquired it for a couple of grand in 1972. It featured it in the odd show between then and 1975 without attracting too much attention.

But then it all kicked off following an article in the Sunday Times in February 1976.

Journalist Colin Simpson was less than impressed at some of the work that had been named in the Tate's report of recent purchases.

It's worth pointing out here that the art market is somewhat different in 2019 than it was in the mid-70s when publicly funded museums were the primary buyers of contemporary art in the UK.

Arts funding has been scaled back, and it is now incumbent on private collectors, notably the influential Charles Saatchi, to gamble on (or shape) which art will be worth anything the future by spending their own money.

On the receiving end of Simpson's *chagrin* were contemporary works by the (sometimes) confrontational East London duo, Gilbert and George and Claes Oldenburg, the sculptor and *pre-pop* 'godfather' of Pop Art. But the real focus of his resentment was this Carl Andre chap.

And 'his bricks'.

Such was his displeasure, the rattled Simpson can't even bring himself to refer to the work by its title, *Equivalent VIII*. Throughout his tirade it is only ever 'the bricks'. The writer is inferring that the Tate had somehow been hoodwinked into buying the bricks from Andre in some sort of elaborate great *brick'n'roll* swindle.

The cause was then taken up by the British tabloids, who love only a few things more than reporting on the possibility that experts and boffins were being duped! And that good public money was being thrown after bad!

So, is it art?

Or just a pile of bricks pretending to be art?

Equivalent VIII is one of a series of eight.

Each of the works is composed of 120 identical bricks stacked two high and placed directly on the gallery floor.

Although the eight works in the series are *equivalents* in many respects, not least the number of bricks, each is unique in its *configuration*.

Equivalent V, for example, is five lengths long and twelve widths wide, while Equivalent VIII measures ten by six. And so on.

Aside from The Tate's acquisition of *VIII* none of the other *Equivalent* series sold at the time, and so Andre took the bricks back to the Long Island Brickworks Co, from where the materials had initially been procured and got his money back. He recreated the works for a retrospective in 1969, this time using firebricks. The original sand-lime bricks were no longer available as Long Island Brickyard had closed down. Whether its slack returns policy was a contributory factor is unknown.

An instance of *Equivalent VIII* is now preserved for eternity in the Tate (post)Modern.

VIII is boring to look at, easily repeatable. It's not even made of a material associated with fine art, like bronze or marble.

Yet the publicity it generated has ensured it is one of the most famous works in the Tate collection. And because of its presence in the institution of the gallery, it is, de facto, a work of art.

In galleries under the spell of postmodernist philosophy - *The Artworld* - artworks are anything that the museums or galleries decide to show us, it is *up to* the rest of us, the plebs, to keep step with the *circumambient weltanschauung*.

Pay attention at the back!

'Works of art don't mean anything.'

But to be fair Andre is a minimalist, rather than a *conceptual* artist, and so he would say that.

There is a big difference.

Conceptual art replaces paintings and sculptures with ideas, it's purely intellectual.

If, as Andre says, *Equivalent VIII* means *nothing*, then it's not conceptual. There is literally no idea there, and since it doesn't even resemble anything other than what it is – a pile of bricks –

then that's all it is. So, it's not even *postmodernist?*

But it is in a gallery, so it must be art?

It is what *it is not*, yet it is what *it is*.

The year after the 'bricks' kerfuffle, the Tate launched one of its most enduring public appeals. Two paintings by the great 18th century English *landscape-with-horses* artist George Stubbs were set to be sold to a foreign collector. The two pictures, *Haymakers* and *Reapers*, would be lost to Britain's art public unless the Tate could raise the necessary two hundred grand.

People got behind this one, Lotteries and competitions boosted the coffers alongside contributions from businesses and trusts.

In a radio interview with the Tate Director, Norman Reid, asking for competition prizes to boost the fundraising effort, the terms and conditions for contributors were laid out.

Any prize in the lottery was required by law to be worth no more than two thousand pounds.

At the time, drive-away cost of a brand-new Mini Cooper car was just under the two-grand threshold.

The next day two Minis were delivered to the back door of the Tate, one donated by an oil firm president, another from a national car dealership.

The two prizes were proudly displayed in the sculpture galleries.

If you've been following along thus far, then remember what we have already established. It is the *institution of the gallery* that defines the work of art.

But Carl Andre has already stated that sculpture should *define* rather than simply *occupy* space. Indeed, it should *eliminate the division* between artistic and ordinary space.

If he'd not been so quick to return his bricks to the vendor, then they could have been flogged to the Tate to *define a space* to house the Minis in the Stubbs appeal.

Equivalent IX, a garage.

It turns out that the people like pictures of landscapes and horses. The appeal quickly hit the target, and the paintings were saved for the nation.

Perhaps inspired by the Stubbs appeal (not really), a couple of New York-based Russian artists, Vitaly Komar and Alex Melamid were planning their own 'conceptual' art experiment back in the mid-1990s they began with a slightly unusual first step.

The artists appointed a market research firm - *Martila & Kiley* of Boston - to run surveys aimed at uncovering the aesthetic preferences and tastes in painting in over a dozen countries and report back with the hard data.

The goal was to find out if a real 'people's art' could be defined, and if so, what that might look like. When the results of these surveys were revealed, the dynamic duo would make as many paintings as necessary – guided by the data - to reflect the results. The resulting artworks were to be billed as *'Most Wanted'*.

In contrast, they would also produce paintings to reflect the 'least wanted', based on the attributes that polled the worst.

Melamid described their concept for the project in this way:

In a way, it was a traditional idea, because faith in numbers is fundamental to people...in ancient Greece when sculptors wanted to create an ideal human body, they measured the most beautiful men and women. They then made an average measurement. In a way, this is the same thing; in principle, it's nothing new.

It's interesting: we believe in numbers, and numbers never lie. Numbers are innocent. It's absolutely true data. It doesn't say anything about personalities, but it says something more about ideals, and about how this world functions. That's really the truth, as much as we can get to the truth. Truth is a number.

The results were fascinating. In just about every one of the 12 or so countries polled, the data revealed the 'same' favourite – the *most wanted.*

Almost universally popular were attributes adding up to a painting of some kind of landscape, viewed from a raised position and featuring a few human figures going about their business. With some animals in the foreground (horses were popular), with a big blue sky and some coastline or a path extending into the distance. And some water - a river, the sea or a lake.

Just about every country wanted this configuration. Only the Italians deviated slightly, although the ideal was still heavily *figurative*, and the researchers put some of the anomalies down to an error in the sampling making it, perhaps, marginally unrepresentative.

And almost universally rejected by the people – the *least wanted* - were abstract compositions, featuring geometric or angular shapes.

(That's not to say non-figurative or non-narrative painting can't still be appealing. Humans have a permanent innate taste for virtuoso displays of creativity. Spectacular giant Pollocks or the Rothko room at the Tate, for example. Rothko was heavily influenced by Michelangelo's Laurentian Library in Florence.)

But does science have an explanation for why anyone should claim to enjoy 'conceptual' art or participating in *art-speak?*

Just as biology can explain why we have a greater fear of snakes than fear of cars, so it also may tell why it's easier for us (secretly) to appreciate a beautiful landscape more than an arrangement of bricks.

But it's not a simple as that in the world of human interaction, where almost all of our consumption is competitive.

This need evolved long before brands and products existed, and the best brands tap into these evolved needs. Most of the products we buy are purchased to signal our status, intelligence and personality traits to others to advance one or more evolutionary social motives.

The arts themselves are evolutionary adaptations that have prevailed because of their ability to meet the needs necessary for the survival and evolutionary development of humans.

Art is a category that demands high levels of complex abilities in both 'creation' and, just as importantly, appreciation. For the appreciators inside *The Artworld*, the more complicated, the better.

The success of the first Most Wanted project led to many commissions from other countries around the world who wanted their own 'people's choice'. The disappointed artists remarked *'in looking for freedom, we found slavery.'*

It's what the market wants, *comrades*.

The truth is that across all cultures, humans tend to prefer representations - visual experiences - depicting environments where they have; a vista, an advantage in height, an open terrain, diverse vegetation and a nearby body of water.

Because a landscape such as this was ideal survive-and-thrive habitat for our ancestors who lived on the African Savannah.

This could be described as a kind of Darwinian aesthetics. And shines another light on writing, movies, music and painting by showing how their character is connected to prehistoric preferences and interests.

Komar and Melamid should not be too concerned. Once every territory has their *people's* choice then there will still a big-spending market of virtue-signallers looking for difficult *Post-Art Nostalgic Socialist Realism*.

Because it is *signals* first, *product* second.

These kinds of pieces may typically end up hanging in a cavernous apartment in a block overlooking Central Park in New York or Hyde Park in London – at the time of writing there's a nice one on the Bayswater Road on the market for 18.5 million, this kind of accommodation, and vista don't come cheap...

What would Arthur Danto think?

Remember, the philosopher and postmodern art theorist of *The Artworld* fame?

He suggests that the results of the *'Most Wanted'* experiment should be disregarded and were most likely a by-product of the hideous worldwide 'calendar' industry. This includes art print reproductions, poster shops, the picture section in IKEA and the basic philistinism of the *numbnut proles*, incapable and unfit to discern what only *The Artworld* can.

Far more likely is that it is not the *calendar industry* [sic] that conspired to influence taste, but rather its products cater to universal, deep-rooted, prehistoric, innate human preferences.

(Aesthetic taste is an evolutionary trait, and as such, it is shaped by natural selection.)

It's possible that reason the bulk of postmodern political art fails to break out of *The Artworld* bubble and connect with ordinary punters is that it is too heavy on *ideology* but too light on *ideas*.

But what about postmodern advertising?

In 2010 a group of academics and researchers led by Georgios Zotos from the Aristotle University School of Economics in Greece conducted a study of over 1500 US Super Bowl commercials going back to 1969 and through to 2009.

The team concluded that the use of *postmodern* advertising *devices* had increased significantly during the last four decades. The researchers identified these elements as surreal visuals, symbolic associations and humorous juxtapositions. Whereas what they define as 'modern' advertising approaches - realistic visuals, the use of expert testimonial and high levels of informational content - has reduced.

Students of advertising will consider these basic findings somewhat banal – the story of the 'creative revolution' of the late '60s is well documented.

When standard American car ads sold speed, performance and design, the DDB 'Think Small' campaign for the VW Beetle went in completely the opposite direction.

Smart, witty and self-deprecating the Volkswagen ads also went in the opposite direction to the dominant school of the 1950s (*modern*) advertising, basically the Rosser Reeves philosophy.

'Each advertisement must make a proposition to the consumer. Not just words, not just product puffery, not just show-window advertising. Each advertisement must say to each reader: Buy this product, and you will get this specific benefit'.

With 'Think Small' consumers were now being trusted to be smart enough to work things out for themselves. To 'know' it was an ad. And to know that the advertiser knows that they know it.

But digging into the findings of Zotos and co, the more significant shift is one further towards *reflexivity*. A tendency for the inclusion of *self-conscious* and self-*contradictory* qualities, in particular, the use of pastiche and, occasionally, parody.

(Parody is distinct from pastiche. Unlike pastiche which *celebrates* the work it imitates, parody *mocks*. Oasis, on occasions, was a *pastiche* of the Beatles, whereas the Rutles is exclusively *parody*. And more confusingly, a *double-ironic quotation*, the movie itself was co-produced by George Harrison – a Beatle.)

This contradictory stance - ironic quotation or appropriation - is best described as *intertextuality*. Meaning the shaping of a *text's* meaning by another *text*.

Parody, for example, is doubly-coded, *intertextual*. It legitimises and subverts at the same time. Like saying something and at the same time putting quote marks around what is being said. Even ironic becomes 'ironic'.

It was clearly in this spirit, that the board-game company Cards against Humanity produced a 'Super Bowl ad', directly mocking Super Bowl advertising for the 2017 big game.

A 30-second silent film of a single potato with

the word 'Advertisement' written on it.

Accompanying the video was a press release claiming that the company had bankrupted itself by buying a $500,000 spot – it clearly had not - and a long-winded ad-mocking *manifesto*.

Given that rebellious craft beer company BrewDog – of Punk IPA fame – come from the same part of the world as me I'm hesitant to be too critical of the (much-lauded by adland insiders) 2019 'Advert' campaign, which took the same approach.

The 'knowing' campaign basically features a pack shot and the word 'advert'. It ran on TV – in the mega-rating Game of Thrones breaks – on billboards and on the sides of buses.

'We don't want to live in a world dominated by bad beer any more than you want to live in one with lame advertising', went the party-line.

So, their advertising was deliberately 'lame'. And heavy on the *self-reflexivity*. But, to be fair, what else could they do?

The problem was that - echoing the same Banksy

line that turned into a banana skin for the artist - BrewDog had repeatedly ranted an anti-advertising rhetoric. '[Advertising] is the antithesis of everything we stand for and everything we believe in. It's a medium that is shallow, it's fake, and we want nothing to do with it.'

Adding that they would rather *set fire to their money than spend it on advertising*.

Unlike the KLF, they didn't burn it.

It wasn't their money to toast, in any case. It most likely came from the private equity firm who had just injected £213m into the operation and weren't going to hang about for their return.

At the same time as the 'punk' anti-advertising 'advertising' was on air, their investors lawyers were (allegedly) sending cease-and-desist letters to a pub in 'Brum called *Lone Wolf* (it's a trademark owned by BrewDog) as well as (allegedly) trying to take out another bar for using just for using 'punk' in its name.

Death or glory becomes just another story.

The post-punk *reflexivity* comes cheekily full

circle. 'Advert' is reminiscent of the 1986 PIL 'Album' (also known as *Compact Disc* or *Cassette* depending on the format you got).

Big business is very wise,
I'm inside free enterprise.

Ironically, the overly political material most associated with postmodern*ist* advertising is not postmodern in this sense. It is closer to the *modern* approach that postmodernism is supposed to have replaced. It is conspicuous by the almost complete absence of *intertextuality* or quotation while its messages, stripped of creative wordplay, come straight out of postmodern*ist* theory.

Ads that underestimate the intelligence of consumers are immediately at risk of falling flat.

Berating your customers for not being good enough is even more risky, as Gillette found out to their cost with *'The Best A Man Can Be'* debacle. In a rush to align the brand with millennial market, Gillette and their agencies bought into so-called market 'research' claiming that young people wanted to buy from brands that demonstrate corporate social responsibility. Gillette naturally went after *cause-du-jour*, 'toxic masculinity', in a bid to score some points.

It all got a bit *bristly* as the urge to make a political statement overtook the consideration of some of the basic building blocks needed to make effective advertising. They forgot what they were supposed to be doing.

Behavioural economics nerds would have immediately spotted the negative social proof blunder, sometimes known as *norm muddling*. While Gillette clearly disapproves of the many *bad* male behaviours (mansplaining, bullying and harassment, etc.) the spot reveals, it simultaneously suggests that these behaviours are widespread and popular amongst all men.

A schoolboy/girl error. Rule number one of behaviour change club is 'make the desired behaviours appear to be the prevalent norm'.

(Yes, there can be exceptions to this rule, but this case is not one of them).

But the biggest problem was that it just wasn't very creative. Big on *ideology*, short on *an idea*.

If it was as easy as just telling people to buy a product or service and they will do so, there would be no need for an advertising industry. Likewise, just telling people not to do bad behaviours is never going to fly.

Even Ogilvy and Reeves thought that consumers needed a modicum of persuasion!

That other stalwart of men's grooming, Old Spice, probably did a lot more for the cause on their relaunch in 2011 - and with mascot Isaiah Mustafa in tow. By poking fun at stereotypes of masculinity in a creative way that gave the audience some credit for intelligence.

However, what mainstream advertisers are slowly coming around to; is the new logic of postmodern advertising - the *pseudo-event*.

The historian Daniel Boorstin's book, *The Image: A Guide to Pseudo-Events in America*, was first published in 1962. In it, Boorstin coined the term *pseudo-event* to describe the modern news cycle, but it became more of postmodern prophecy.

Boorstin defines *The Image* as a spectacle. The media event that *creates news* rather than being simply *reported*.

In 2019 the pseudo-event retains and expands on its four original principal attributes:

1. It is not spontaneous but comes about because it has been planned, planted, or incited.

2. Is planted primarily for the immediate purpose of being reported or reproduced. Therefore, its occurrence is *arranged for the convenience* of social media and news media. Success is measured by how widely it is published and replicated. *The question 'Is it real?' is less important than 'Is it newsworthy?'*

3. Its relation to the underlying reality of the situation is ambiguous. Without this ambiguity, a pseudo-event cannot be very interesting.

4. Usually, it is intended to be a self-fulfilling prophecy.

(Through this lens it's hard not to view the entirety of the Trump presidency as one long pseudo-event, likewise Meghan and Harry.)

Of course, there are big differences between the nature of media in the Boorstin 1960s and the nature of media today.

Not least, the fact that media in the 1960s wasn't *real-time* media. If anyone wanted to spread a message, they had the options of radio, television or printed material.

Or else take it to the streets.

These media would transmit that message at their own time, not instantly.

Today, media is both interactive and real-time, specifically social media.

Events happen in space and time that is shaped by the available media - the perfect conditions for the *pseudo-event*.

When KFC ran out of chicken and had to apologise to their customers, they took out full-page press ads in newspapers.

For this reason alone, the apology could be 'trusted' to a degree. It's the extravagance of the gesture that can contribute to advertising effectiveness by increasing credibility.

You have to put your money where your mouth is. Press ads are expensive, and consumers intuitively know this.

But KFC's apology was a *pseudo-event*, explicitly designed to get traction in other news media and on Twitter. The underlying situation was ambiguous. Did they really run out of chicken?

Nike's *Kaepernick* poster, Gillette, *Fearless Girl*, Brewdog's *Advert* and countless others are all *pseudo-events*.

Arranged for the convenience of social media and news media.

Whereas reach could once be bought it now must be obtained. By being reported and replicated.

The rules have changed, but the game remains the same. As we used to say back in *ye olden days* of social media; *if it doesn't spread, its dead.*

Italian sculptor and installation artist Maurizio Cattelan had a reputation for being a bit of a wag on the contemporary scene. Outside of the *Artworld* bubble no-one else knew of him, until 2019.

Cattelan's *Comedian*, as everyone now knows, is the banana, duct-taped to a wall.

Borrowing the language of start-ups, the work is now being called 'the unicorn of the art world'.

Being good in business is indeed the most fascinating kind of art, Andy...

If postmodern advertising acts primarily as publicity (not persuasion) so too *Comedian* was pure publicity for Maurizio's brand rather than an artwork. And it was both.

Now half the world knows his name.

Of course, one thing that *anti-advertising* advertising can't deny is its own *conflictedness*. It is an integral part of the system it claims to oppose. It 'reinforces' as much as it 'subverts' the conventions it claims to challenge. And is entirely complicitous with the values it 'calls into question'.

However, the creative advertising in postmodernity – *ironic* and *indirect* - makes its working elements more visible. A kind of *operational transparency*, making it useful to consumers despite the contradictions.

It sends an economic *signal* that helps us to make pretty accurate inferences about the quality and value of a brand.

'While we have given others great powers to deceive us, to create pseudo-events, celebrities and images, they could not have done so without our collaboration.' – Boorstin

(Products are products. People know what they are. The brand itself *is the quality*.)

It was in the *modern* paradigm that the consumer occupied a fixed position, as a *target*, receiving messages driven at them.

In this respect *targeting* - despite being *technologically* advanced, is not only cheap and nasty (in effect, *the real anti-advertising)* but also fundamentally out of step with the age...

SOMETHING'S GONE WRONG AGAIN...

And again, and again,
And again, again...

THE YELLOW TANG IS A brightly coloured fish that can be found swimming in the tropical reefs of the Indian Ocean.

When the Tang needs its gills to be cleaned, the fish looks for its pal, the Cleaner Wrasse who can be recognised by its bright electric blue colour and black stripe that runs down the length of its body.

Cleaner Wrasses hang around in 'cleaning stations'. The Carwash in the reef, like in the movie *Shark Tale*.

The Wrasse is given access to the Tang's gills and mouth. Then it eats any parasites and dead tissue off of the skin of its 'client' in a relationship that provides food and protection for the Wrasse, and considerable health benefits for the Tang. A reciprocal situation. A symbiosis.

To gain access to the big fish, the Cleaner Wrasse must first win the Tang's trust. To do this, it performs a kind of secret *dance* – this represents a special 'code' that the host understands. The marine equivalent of a powerpoint presentation of its credentials and category experience at a chemistry meeting.

This system typically works out fine, and it is this implicit symbiosis agreement between two species that satisfies both partners that each is indispensable and the mutual advantage is obvious.

But there are *cheaters* about, some other fish that *mimic* Cleaner Wrasses. For example, a particular species of Blenny called *Aspidontus Taeniatus* has evolved the ability to perform a pretty good impersonation the same behaviour.

It is almost identical in size and appearance to the Cleaner Wrasse. It even sports the same shiny stripe down its back and lurks around near the same reefs watching and waiting.

If approached by a Yellow Tang, the deceptive Blenny also knows the secret code. The secret dance that will get it access.

This fella's powerpoint presentation is impressive, but ultimately pure deception. It bamboozles the Tang, perhaps with 25 slides about how Gen Z demand personalised communications and authentic relationships with purpose-driven fish. Either way, the *infelicitous* Tang is fooled, Blenny is good to go, and the deception is complete.

Once allowed in, instead of providing a cleaning service, the rogue Blenny uses its super sharp teeth to rip chunks of flesh from the hapless client.

Rather than ridding his client of parasites, Blenny *IS* the parasite. But cleverly disguised.

They know the codes, the moves, they know which kinds of secret dances will get them access to the big fish. And there are lots of them.

Bullshit is much harder to detect when we want to agree with it, and the Tang wants to believe it.

As the biologist Robert Trivers found in his landmark work on deceit and self-deception, straight-up honesty (*sucker*) is not always evolutionarily stable. It is easily displaced by deception (*cheat*) which, in turn, forms a new equilibrium.

Deception is, indeed, the new equilibrium in the prevailing marketing technology *lumascape.*

Adtech was supposed to be the silver bullet of efficiency that would solve Wanamaker's famous dilemma of '*half the money I spend on advertising is waste, the problem is I don't know which half.*'

Advertisers who choose *to target* are usually not being deliberately deceptive. And to state that it is full of fraud and a vector for malware is banal, as is the claim that all of the ad money will inevitably migrate over to digital.

However, an environment that facilitates this kind of targeting also facilitates deceptive communication, by default. There's further deception as brands still naively believe they're placing ads in real media. At the same time, the ad systems they pay are just chasing eyeballs to any place they go, undermining the brand value of all the media it uses.

The cutest deceptive stroke was the rebranding of 'behavioural targeting' as 'performance.'

Something that creates next to no value rebranded as though it was the ultimate in value. Who wouldn't buy 'media' that performs? For an industry that consistently celebrates the death of 'traditional' advertising and brand value that was a genius stroke of branding.

If that's not enough, disguised as 'advertising', the new adtech environment has incentivised publishers to prioritise 'content' over journalism giving 'fake news' a business model. Hey, clickbait is easier to produce than the real news, and the deceived will pay *anybody* for *any eyeballs*.

But all of this is not important.

It's all innovation, right?

Today, what constitutes 'good advertising' is that which appears to be the *most innovative (this means only technology)*. So agencies are rearranging themselves around a very thin version of what innovation could look like.

2018's chiefmartec.com adtech *lumascape*

actually charts 7,040 marketing technology solutions from over 6,000 unique marketing technology vendors.

While that represents just 3% growth from 2018 (compared to 27% growth from 2017's 5,381 solutions), the scale and velocity of growth in this space over the last 10 years are staggering.

In fact, the size of the 2018 landscape was equivalent to all of the marketing tech landscapes from 2011 through 2016 added together. Indeed, in 2011 they numbered just 150.

And this is just the legit stuff.

But the elephant in the room is this. At the core of many of these companies' operations are the exact same technologies that make ad fraud possible—and inevitable – so much so that it's the number two source of revenue for international organised crime after narcotics, fact fans, and it's priced into the market.

A good liar has a significant advantage in a world unaccustomed to lies. And when there's big-dollar to be got, not much wonder we're in an ecosystem rife with manipulation, fraud, and scams.

They look a bit like something to do with advertising, they can talk a language that's a bit like the language of advertising, we've fallen for it.

Ignorance can be bliss until you are outwitted and out-hacked. My good friend Don Marti sums it up like this; 'when marketers challenge domestic terrorist hackers and fraud hackers to a hacking contest [they will always] come in third'.

But the machine is broke,
Something's gone wrong again...

A business *concept* is the basic idea of a business. It includes information such as what company actually does - the service or product - the market for those things, and some sort of proposition that positions a company relative to competitors.

The ad agency model was once reasonably straightforward. Agencies were essentially competing on *competence* around a bunch of generic category benefits.

Increasingly, of course, agencies have begun to promise an additional combination of strategic, technological and management consulting services as part of the *concept*. So much so, that media and advertising issues are put in a broader, business-oriented perspective and agencies claim to offer *much, much more* than just creative or planning and buying.

In fact, what used to be core competencies are presented as almost a side-show to the idea of business consulting!

For employees, this can be a far more attractive picture, compared to being 'only' into advertising or media. However, the extent to which the actual activities of the business aligned with the new business concept is mostly negligible.

Very few advertising agency foot soldiers will have ever been near an Enterprise technology IBM or one of the 'big 4' professional services firms, they don't have that kind of *competence*. But that doesn't mean that there's not a strong receptiveness among ad people for descriptions that give the impression of an *upgrading of activities* into something much more impressive.

And there's the other *ad fraud* problem.

This is not the one with bots, click-farms and app-spoofing but the rise of social media - LinkedIn in particular - has meant that there are many more 'voices' out there, pushing their own personal brands and agendas.

Advertising and media have our own cult of celebrity. For many, the conference circuit is pretty much a full-time job for *bullshitters*.

To the bullshitter, right and wrong matters not. True or false matters not. What matters is that *you are paying attention*. Or as Harry Frankfurt famously noted 'It's not important to [the bullshitter] what the world really is like. What is important is how he'd like to represent himself.' Although the booming industry for bullshitters is not limited to men only.

Bullshit is a two-way street, of course. It requires both *bullshitter* and *bullshitee*.

(When people judge as profound what they have failed to grasp, *obscurity inspires awe*.)

The bullshitter quotes other people (who quote other people), and the quotes can be traced back in a *recursive loop*.

The bullshitter is not interested in helping anyone solve any business problems, typically they are only interested in building their own thought leader profile.

Sean Blanda is credited with coining the *Bullshit Industrial Complex* on the Adobe Design blog.

Essentially, BIC describes how too many people are pushing their opinions on topics, not because they know and understand the issues, but because they've read about them, from someone else, who was quoting someone else.

Blanda outlines the bullshit industrial complex as a pyramid of groups that goes like this:

Group 1: People actually generating ideas, launching businesses, doing creative work, taking risks and sharing first-hand learnings.

Group 2: People writing about group 1 in clear, concise, accessible language.

...... the line of bullshit demarcation here......

Group 3: People aggregating the learnings of group 2, passing it off as first-hand wisdom.

Group 4: People aggregating the learnings of

group 3, believing they are as worthy of praise as the people in group 1.

Groups 5+: And downward....

The complex eventually becomes a fully-fledged self-sufficient ecosystem when people in group 4 are reviewing books by people in group 3 who are only tweeting people in group 2 who are appearing on the podcasts started by people in group 3.

Before you start, I know this *was* me. And yes, I only wrote my first book to try and get more speaking gigs at conferences.

Didn't happen though, I'm not enough of a futurist and can't even get enough Group 4's to quote me out of Group3...

The digital era is remarkably similar to 'The Renaissance' (1350–1600) in one respect. Both periods produced favourable conditions for charlatans. Old ways of thinking were cast aside, and it seemed that anything was possible.

In her wonderful exploration of the origins and history of the American Medicine Show, *'Snake Oil,*

Hustlers and Hambones', Ann Anderson discerned:

A semiliterate village dweller might have been aware of a new discovery, but he or she was probably not sufficiently educated to distinguish fact from fiction. Charlatans could not have flourished without the support of a willing, naïve audience.

The extraordinary power of impostors is therefore only to be understood after a consideration of the minds and circumstances of their gullible victims, the crowds who sought them out, half-convinced before a word was spoken.

If charlatans had not existed, villagers would have invented them.'

Environments that present these conditions are almost perfect settings for the cultivation and distribution of bullshit, of course.

Author and Professor of Organisational Behaviour at Cass Business School Andre Spicer calls them *neocracies*.

A *neocracy* is an organisation which is organised

around the 'constant generation of newness. The central purpose is the continued reorganisation, metamorphosis and transformation of itself.'

The question of why all the transformation is taking place is a side issue, the only important thing is that the change is happening, and is continuous and future-obsessed. Questions about dealing with the realities of the present - and lessons that can be learned from the past are of no importance.

Even referring to historical lessons - or facts - is often seen as being 'traditional, 'stuck in the *Madmen* era' or just simply 'negativity'.

(Positivity, of course, means unbridled enthusiasm for any new idea, regardless of how stupid or impractical.)

It follows naturally that the *neocrats* themselves will usually be people who can't claim authority through any formal education, or even having any basic knowledge of the industry or any significant experience in the trenches.

If anything, these things are usually seen as a disadvantage.

The only things that matter are *pivoting towards transformation, reinventing experiences* and – the perennial - *disruption*! All with scant understanding of why, and even *scanter* interest in consequences.

Spicer also points out that it is *critical* in these perpetual change endeavors to ensure that everyone forgets how change initiatives have failed in the past. For this reason, bringing the consultants in is naturally an optimum strategy.

Fresh eyes can more easily repeat old mistakes!

The *illusion of the broken system* states that any system is the way it is because the people with the most leverage want it that way.

The proponents of these superior *innovations* are unable to distinguish themselves through creative talent since they have next to none. And so each new 'innovation' takes advertising further from its original purpose and further into *nothing*.

The fetishisation of technology for its own sake (over creativity) by the untalented.

But brands are complex abstractions.

Creative advertising had made it possible for consumers to make some sense of these convoluted concepts.

But because the schema of *what-is-advertising* has now been so twisted out of recognition, it cannot fulfil this need.

And now, because the people who need to be reached have started to ignore and block this kind of advertising, they don't even remember, or credit, the role advertising ever performed in culture.

This situation doesn't add up to an evolutionarily stable strategy. Successful adaptive changes build on the past rather than chucking it out wholesale, successful adaptations are both conservative and progressive.

They make the best possible use of previous wisdom while continually experimenting on the edges to see what might work in the future.

In biological adaptations, though DNA changes may have far-reaching effects on survival and reproductive success for the individuals within a group that inherit the new DNA, the actual amount of DNA that changes is tiny.

(Homo sapiens DNA differs from Chimpanzees by only about 2%)

A challenge for innovators then, is not so much what to throw out but what to retain, and how to riff on that.

Instead, and just like Rauschenberg's erased De Kooning which occupies space that could have been used to present real art, the new 'advertising' occupies space that should contain real advertising.

And more worrying is this.

It becomes more and more accepted that this new definition of advertising IS the advertising.

If perhaps the German philosopher—and darling of the postmodern*ists*—Martin Heidegger had been the head of an advertising agency (rather than a part- time Nazi and ponderer of *ontological hermeneutics*) he might well have offered up this explanation - 'every [ad], so far as it is an [ad], is made out of nothing.'

Any system is the way it is because the people with the most leverage want it that way. But at the moment what we have is just the appearance of a *functional system.*

We are continually failing to distinguish between real advertising and what are not just sub-standard versions of advertising, but the products of the *destroyers* of advertising.

It is not even conceptual. At least Duchamp had the decency to make up some semi-comprehensible bullshit to go along with his urinal—*to shift the focus of art from physical craft to intellectual interpretation.*

After abandoning reason and logic, after experiencing real boredom and terrifying dread, we unveil the final mystery of mysteries: Nothing. —Hicks.

You now the scene, it's very humdrum.

The journalist Paul Morley once said *'Buzzcocks came from the better side of punk, the bands who were aware of things like Faust and Can.'*

He wasn't wrong.

By early 1976, and after building his own *oscillator* from scratch, Bolton Institute of Technology engineering student Pete Shelley had already completed a whole 'album' of experimental synth music, inspired by his love of Kraftwerk and other *krautrock* bands.

It was there that he first met brainy weirdo Howard Devoto who was looking for someone to soundtrack an art movie he'd made. Howard was studying philosophy down the road.

Both Pete and Howard were avid NME readers and after reading a small review of relatively unknown London band, Sex Pistols, and inspired by a quote in the piece attributed to Pistols guitarist Steve Jones (*'we're not into music, we're into chaos'*), the new friends booked a small room at Manchester Free Trade Hall and invited the Pistols to play.

This event June 1976 has gone down in history as 'the gig that changed the world' (among the 30 or 40 misfits in the audience were future members of Joy Division/New Order, The Smiths and The Fall.)

The day after the show the pair immediately formed Buzzcocks and booked the Pistols to play again six weeks later with their own combo as support. At the second gig, the hall was full to its

150 capacity.

The rest is history, of course.

Billy Bragg once remarked that if everyone who claimed to have seen the Pistols in '76 really had they would have sold out a month at Wembley Stadium rather than a few one-nighters at assorted Soho strip clubs. Correspondingly, if everyone who claimed to be at one of the Manchester shows had attended it would have been a week of sell-outs at the G-Mex.

(If every ad planner and marketer who claim in-depth knowledge of Ehrenberg-Bass principles had bought '*How Brands Grow*' then I reckon Byron and co would be kicking back on a private island next to the ones occupied by Richard Branson and assorted retired Bond villains rather than still pursuing their academic careers.)

Paul Morley is also on record as claiming 'I remember delightedly screaming, *this is like...Ornette Coleman* when I went to see the early Buzzcocks play.'

(But he was now just being a bit silly, albeit setting the tone for much of his subsequent writing.)

Shelley's iconic *deliberately inane* minimal two-note guitar solo in *Boredom* (from Buzzcocks debut EP *Spiral Scratch*) was pretty *conceptual.*

The solo consisted of just two notes repeated 66 times, ending with a single *modulated seventh.* One suspects that it was this last flourish that Morley interpreted as the *free-jazz* component.

Pete played a Starway, a cheap Japanese brand of guitar sold in department stores.

A rudimentary instrument, the Starway featured just one pickup and two control dials for volume and tone.

Shelley is said to have bought his in a Manchester branch of Woolworths.

(While the guitars were sold there, Pete actually acquired his one - second-hand - in a charity shop.)

To be more exact, all of the four tracks on '...*Scratch*' were recorded using just TWO-THIRDS of a Starway.

Pete had accidentally smashed his axe into two pieces during a rehearsal.

The top part of the body snapped off. However, the guitar was still totally playable, and so continued to be his primary tool until the band had a few hits and he could afford to upgrade to the (only marginally more sophisticated) Gibson Marauder.

If inspiring the DIY punk *revolution* with only two-thirds of a guitar was not minimal enough for you, Shelley's engineering chops learned back at Bolton Tech came in handy.

It's often been said that creativity can be propelled by constraints - even if the limits are artificial.

He rewired the insides of the Starway to bypass the volume and tone dials, sending the pickup direct to the jack - it was now two-thirds of a guitar with only ONE sound. It was a pretty good sound, though.

The economist Ernst Friedrich 'Fritz' Schumacher once coined the term *appropriate technology*. Meaning the 'simplest level of technology that can achieve the intended purpose'.

Simplicity has never been a bad idea.

In a world of applied *appropriate advertising technology*, most of the links in our complicated and bloated demand/supply chain - SSPs, DSPs, exchanges, third-party verification systems and various proprietary reporting mechanisms - wouldn't even have a business. They wouldn't exist.

So-called 'safety' tech vendors have even more mysterious incentives given that they DEPEND on the continued existence of botnets, domain-spoofers and malware fraudsters for their own business model.

But when every step in a web ad 'value' chain is deliberately opaque, they all do to some extent. A cynic would call it a suspicious exercise in deliberate obfuscation.

The funny thing is that we think we know how this advertising technology demand/supply chain works, and the more available information we have, the more our confidence grows.

The Illusion of Explanatory Depth (or IOED) – is the persistent illusion people have that we know more about more than we actually do.

IOED was coined in 2002 by cognitive scientists

Rozenblit and Keil.

Rozenblit and Keil asked people to rate their knowledge of how mundane mechanisms worked – things like zippers, refrigerators and toilets.

Respondents rated their comprehension highly, but when pressed to explain their understanding, they tended to fail miserably.

IOED is pervasive primarily because we have access to almost infinite amounts of information, but consume it only superficially.

Why bother, we can just read the tweets and soundbites?

The apparent technological sophistication inherent to the current paradigm also offers a *veneer of profundity*.

Or *pseudo-profound bullshit*, if you prefer. Seemingly impressive assertions that are presented as true and meaningful but are actually vacuous.

Where there's a mystery, there's a margin.

Fritz Schumacher also famously said; *'Any intelligent fool can make things bigger, more complex, and more violent. It takes a touch of genius—and a lot of courage to move in the opposite direction.'*

But as the number of businesses mediating between advertisers and publishers (and the agency) grows - all claiming to do *something* - and as 70 cents in every dollar gets eaten up by whatever that something is, we've never been further from *sending the pickup direct to the jack.*

BLURB

A FORTY SECOND PLAY
BY TENZING SCOTT BROWN

BLURB

It involves two characters.

They are The Man and Bill Drummond.

They are sitting next to each other on the crowded top deck of the Clapham omnibus.

There may also be a third character.

The Man:

Well I think it is the work of an opinionated white male of a certain age.

Bill Drummond:

It takes one to know one.

The Man:

That is no excuse.

Bill Drummond:

Well none-the-less, I think his opinions expressed in this book are worthy opinions even if like mine they are the opinions of...

The Ticket Inspector:

Can I see your pass?

Bill Drummond:

I'm afraid that I have left mine at home.

The Ticket Inspector:

Then I will have to politely ask you to exit the bus at the next stop.

The Man:

But we...

The Ticket Inspector:

There are no buts...

But I see you are reading the new book by Eaon Pritchard, I read his last book, I thought it most stimulating. Like a line of speed coursing through the darkest recesses of the brain.

•　•　•　•

Bill Drummond and The Man exit the bus.

The Ticket Inspector continues to inspect tickets in an age when bus tickets no longer exist, even on the top deck of the Clapham omnibus.

The End

CAN YOU COUNT, SUCKERS?

All we have to do is keep up the general truce. We take over one borough at a time.

Secure our territory... secure our turf... Because it's all our turf!

NEVER HOLD A GRUDGE. THIS is what the wellness gurus will tell you. Those kinds of peeves and piques can only ever be self-destructive; they make you bitter and resentful.

Let go of grudges and move on. Leave one's *spleen unvented.* Life is enjoyed by the person who does not carry the burden of past wrongs.

Blah blah blah.

But is that really a good strategy?

For sure, evolutionary time has honed our capacity for forgiveness, this preserves and restores social *aplomb*, but a capacity for anger and self-defence is necessary. It's one practical tactic for safeguarding one's own integrity when faced with the inevitable setbacks, disappointments and treachery of others.

In any case, it's important to tell yourself a coherent story about your own behaviour.

Even if your actual motivations aren't accessible to the mechanisms of your mind that control communication with the outside world, it would make sense for that part put together a decent story about why you did what you did.

Each of us possesses this psychological immune system, it includes various cognitive strategies and distortions that alter how we think about events and people to make them seem less *hawkish*.

Many of these psychological adaptations can be thought of as defensive in nature, they can reshape the meanings of events.

Tolerance, leniency and benevolence are all admirable qualities, but the itchy feeling remains that with each act of forgiveness, there's a danger of looking more like a *sucker*.

In his original, influential paper on reciprocal altruism, the biologist Robert Trivers describes the function of emotions in this way.

They *mediate between our inner calculator and our outer behaviou*r.

Trivers has a mildly eccentric history. Probably the only white scientist to be a getaway driver for the Black Panthers, he's been arrested numerous times, in nick at least once and almost got killed in a *yardie* attack in a Kingston brothel while living on and off in Jamaica since the 70s. And when a couple of machete-wielding burglars had tried to get into his house, he stabbed one of them in the neck.

Not your typical professorial behaviour but the likes of Steven Pinker still reckon him 'one of the great thinkers in the history of Western thought.'

Perhaps his most influential theory - that *self-deception evolved to facilitate the deception of others* – was introduced as an almost off-the-cuff sentence a sentence in the foreword to Richard Dawkins influential 1976 book '*The Selfish Gene*'.

Trivers recalls that he'd planned to flesh out the

theory a bit in a proper paper but didn't get around to it because he was *smoking too much of the herb* at the time.

Trivers points out that the 'emotional' expression of guilt, for example, is useful in helping to repair relationships if you are a *cheater* who's double-crossing has been exposed.

In general, we tend to like people who play fair with us, and on occasions when we get *suckered* by 'unfair' behaviour, then it seems natural to bear a grudge. Adaptive even.

But we may give them a pass if the *guilt* looks impressive enough.

'Why Are People Grudgeful?' was a 1993 nearly-hit for The Fall. Led by cantankerous, authoritarian genius, the late Mark E Smith, the Fall was prolific, pumping out almost an album a year between 1979 and 2017.

Being a Fall member (of which there is legion) was said by many former members to be *character building*. Like doing special forces training.

It wouldn't last long but would be intense and

unpredictable. 12 weeks of physical, mental, and moral terror.

In some agencies I've worked in the experience was akin to being the second guitar in a late 90s Fall line-up.

The record is based on two Jamaican hits from 1968, *'People Funny Boy'* by Lee 'Scratch' Perry, and *'People Grudgeful'* by Joe Gibbs.

Perry had started out in the Jamaican music scene in the late '50s, alongside ska legend Prince Buster, selling records for Clement 'Coxsone' Dodd's Downbeat Sound System.

After a falling out with Dodd, Perry went to work at rival Wirl Records with producer Joe Gibbs.

We have Gibbs to thank for bringing Jamaican stars Max Romeo, Gregory Isaacs and Prince Far I to global audiences under his mentorship.

UK pop-reggae payday eventually came for Joe in '77 with *'Uptown Top Ranking'* by teenagers Althea and Donna, which hit Number 1 in the UK pop charts. Check how we jamming and ting.

Perry was another mercurial character, from a

similar mould as Smith. He now lives and operates his studio in a medieval castle in the Swiss Alps.

Under his guidance, Bob Marley recorded some of his early albums. However, when Perry was alleged to have sold the Wailers' publishing to a UK label, the band acrimoniously dumped him.

Bunny Wailer, still holds a grudge. '[Perry] did nothing for the Wailers, He just sat there in the studio while we played and then he screwed us.'

Perry says, 'I'd rather not talk on Bunny Wailer – he's a miserable person.'

Quelle surprise, it wasn't long until the ever argumentative 'Scratch' also soon fell out with Joe Gibbs and by 1968, he'd left the *Wirl* gig to form his own label, *Upsetter*.

Perry picked up the nickname 'Scratch' after auditioning a singer at Dodds Sound System with a self-penned ditty inspired by a Kingston dance craze, the 'Chicken Scratch'.

The tune went nowhere, but the epithet stuck.

The first release on his new label was '*People Funny Boy*', in effect, a thinly disguised jibe at

Gibbs. Cut on a Monday, mastered on a Tuesday, out on a Wednesday and a hit by Friday.

Why, why people funny bwoy, now that you reach the top an' you turn big shot, all I have done for you, you not remember that.'

In riposte, an indignant Joe marked Scratch down as a *grudger* and retaliated with his 'answer' record *People Grudgeful*; essentially the same tune as '*People Funny...*' with his lyrics taking a bad-tempered swipe back at Perry.

When I was down and out, you didn't help me out, now that I win jackpot, you want to talk about, now that I turn bigshot, you start to chat.

There's an upside to settling arguments in the media, both records were big hits.

For fact fans, both these cuts were probably the first Jamaican pop records to use the slower heavy bass-driven sound that would soon become identified as the reggae *riddim*—a departure from the upbeat ska and rocksteady styles of the day— setting the path towards the pulsing, throb of 70's roots reggae and eventually dub.

Perry ended up with the last laugh, In the subsequent decades, he was to lead from the front in each of the major evolutions in Jamaican music. From his roots in ska and rocksteady, through roots, reggae, dub dancehall, and dubstep.

On release in '76, the Perry produced 'Police & Thieves' sung by Junior Murvin became an underground hit in London, an accidental soundtrack to the Notting Hill Carnival and the accompanying riots that year. This inspired The Clash to record a version for their debut album. Murvin initially hated it, saying *they have destroyed Jah work*!

No *grudges* were held though, the endorsement by punk royalty opened up the original to another audience, propelled it into the UK Top 30 on its re-release, meaning a nice royalty cheque for Junior.

Perry, however, was intrigued by his punk rocker fans. Clash bassist Paul Simonon, in particular, knew the Scratch canon inside out, and so a chance meeting while Perry was in the UK in '77 led to both parties getting together in a studio.

The resulting single *'Complete Control'* gives

Perry the producer credit; however, legend has it that Mick Jones had to stay behind after the sessions to mix out most of Scratch's echo heavy dub treatment for the final version.

(Scratch's recollections of the time are sketchy. While he holds a bit of a *grudge* for not being appropriately paid it's said that he still thinks he was working with the Sex Pistols.)

25 years on from the spat between the producers in Kingston, Mark E. Smith reunited the warring factions in Manchester, England, combining parts of both Perry's and Gibbs' lyrics in the Fall's version, '*Why are People Grudgeful?*'

Of course, Mark E Smith knew a thing or two about grudges.

After forming in 1976, Smith was the only constant member of the Fall. And of the 60-odd musicians who came and went between '76 and the eventual end of the band following Smith's death in 2017, about one third only played in the band for under a year – a new bassist once got fired after a week for ordering salad in a motorway service station - and pretty much no-one came back once they were out.

'One thing I don't do is have people back', Smith explained. 'I've done it once, and it's a real mistake.'

Why are people grudgeful?

Is it a good strategy?

Strategy *games* have existed amongst animals long before humans appeared on the scene employing multiple coexisting strategies, and have been an inspiration for game theorists.

The classic Hawk-Dove Game is perhaps the most well-known example of game theory used in studying animal behaviour.

In this model, we have two individuals that can choose from two strategies when in conflict with one another.

Hawks (the bad guys—always aggressive).

Doves (the good guys—non-aggressive individuals).

Hawks always fight to kill or injure their opponents, whereas the doves will always back off before a fight starts.

In this game, it would be reasonable to predict that doves would quickly become extinct.

Obviously, an all-dove population is not stable since it is always vulnerable to invasion by a hawk. However, an all-hawk population is also unstable since hawks will eventually kill each other.

In any conflict situation, although the dove strategy will always end up losing the resource to a hawk, it will back down before it gets 'killed' in the battle, but if a hawk meets hawk, they fight to the death (or severe injury).

If a hawk meets a dove, dove might mouth off for a bit but then always runs away.

If dove meets dove, there's more mouth until one of them backs down.

So, it seems logical to say that natural selection would appear to favour a mixed population of hawks and doves. But even better, is when participants use a combination of strategies—playing each strategy when appropriate.

This combined hawk-dove strategy is called the *Retaliator*.

Play hawk if you are an owner and a dove if you are an intruder, but turn into a Hawk when you meet another one.

A retaliator would start out playing dove at the beginning of every fight. If the opponent plays hawk and attacks, then he attacks, but if the opponent plays dove, he behaves like a dove.

So, when 2 retaliators meet, they would both behave like doves.

But this means that a retaliator population is still vulnerable to invasion by pure-strategy hawks.

In biology, what is meant by 'strategy' is a pre-programmed, or innate, behavioural policy.

This kind of strategy is not a plan worked out in advance, although the creature behaves as if it were. But it is following a set of hard-wired instructions.

The best strategy/strategies for any individual will be dependent on what the majority of the population are doing, all other individuals will be trying to maximise their own *fitness* too.

In *The Selfish Gene*, Richard Dawkins wondered if there was a better strategy than the theoretical hawk-dove combination and one that corresponds more with observable human behaviour.

Looking first at birds, Dawkins noted that when preening itself a bird can pull off ticks from its own feathers, apart from anything on its own head.

Obviously, it can't reach its head with its own beak, and so the solution is to get a friend to do it, and the bird can pay back the favour later when the other bird needs cleaning.

For this kind of reciprocal arrangement to work, it would be necessary for individual birds to recognise and remember each other as individuals to *keep score*.

If the next day, the original reciprocating bird goes looking for his buddy to get payback, but the first bird turns up his beak and flies off, then he is marked down as a cheat.

Dawkins defines *the cheater* as 'an individual who accepts the benefit of other individuals' altruism, but who doesn't pay it back, or who pays it back insufficiently.'

And our *cheated* feathered friend is now

a *sucker*.

Cheats do better than suckers (*indiscriminate altruists*) because they get the benefits without paying any costs.

Imagine a population consisting of individuals who adopt one of two strategies. *Sucker* vs *Cheat*.

What happens in a situation where these two strategies are in play?

Suckers cooperate with anybody who wants it, indiscriminately, blatant cheats accept help from suckers, but they never cooperate with anybody else, not even somebody who has previously helped them.

Although in this game, let's say most of the cheaters are 'subtle cheats' who appear to be reciprocating — but who always pay back less than they take.

A game theorist designing a test would assign payoff points. The exact values are not essential for the analysis, so long as the benefit payoff of getting is better the cost of giving.

'Any individual *sucker* in a population of

all *suckers* can reckon on being groomed about as often as he grooms.'

The average payoff for a sucker among suckers is therefore positive.'

But now a *cheat* appears in the population.

(In business, *cheater* strategies may be worked out ahead of time. Whereas *sucker* strategies are not really worked out at all.)

For the rest of this argument let's imagine our suckers are a *slow-to-adapt,* multi-billion-dollar industry, and a newer *fast-to-adapt* multi-billion-dollar industry (made up of cheaters) want to get their hands on that revenue.

The relationship between Facebook and Google and media is almost a classic *prisoners dilemma.*

On the one hand, media rely on the big two to distribute their journalism (and ads) to a mass audience. But by doing so, the two tech giants have landed enough *sucker punches* to media that they now control around 70 cents of every dollar spent on digital advertising.

The remaining two-fifths of sod-all is eaten up

by the other platforms like Twitter, the ad tech middleman layer, and whatever is left is split between a multitude of media *suckers* fighting with each other for crumbs.

The problem in the past has been the man turning us against one another.

We have been unable to see the truth because we have fighting for ten square feet of ground, our turf, our little piece of turf.

That's crap, brothers and sisters!

The turf is ours by right.

WE got the streets, suckers! Can you dig it?

Not really. What we have here is a failure to communicate. There are so many players within this game that it's almost impossible to imagine a machination in which they all play together nicely.

The fundamental asymmetry doesn't give the *suckers* much clout when it comes to bargaining. Nothing is broken. It's the illusion of the broken system again. Any system is the way it is because the people with the most leverage want it that way.

For sure, Facebook and Google need news media

and the content they produce to stuff their platforms. But when you own the only distribution channels of any significance, they can easily set media against each another to get whatever suits their own ends.

When you are president(s) of the biggest gang(s) in the city, you don't have to take any shit.

This is the principal advantage in being one of the big cheats in town, and because our suckers really are *suckers*, cheats can count on being 'groomed' by everybody else, but they pay back far less in return.

Cheat's average payoff is consistently a little bit better than the average for the *suckers*.

And cheats are playing the long game.

Cheat *genes* will, therefore, start to spread through the population, more and more cheaters emerge because the payoffs are so high - cheats benefit at the expense of everyone who is trying to do the right thing. And the entire system is set up to reward those who cheat.

Sucker genes will soon be driven to *mergers* and

towards extinction.

No matter what the cheat-to-sucker ratio is in the population, the cheats will always do better than the suckers. Even if the proportion of cheaters reaches 90 per cent penetration and the average payoff for all individuals is next to nothing, the cheats will still be doing better than the suckers.

As the whole game spirals toward extinction, there will never be any time when suckers do better than cheats. The suckers go extinct first, but the cheaters have been smarter, they have *genes* in many other populations.

As long as there are only these two strategies, nothing can stop the extinction of the suckers.

I don't even care if I look a mess,
Don't want to be a sucker like all the rest.

But there's a third strategy.
This one is called *Grudger*.

Grudger is an *extinction rebellion*. Strategic *grudgers* will help out individuals who have previously helped them. Still, if any individual cheats them—or they feel like they've been cheated on—then they will be sure to remember the incident and bear a grudge: they are not going to help that individual in the future.

For grudging to work it would need to be an evolutionarily stable strategy. This is a strategy which, if adopted by most members of a population, can't be beaten by another invading strategy.

On first look, in a population of *grudgers* and *suckers*, it is difficult to tell which is which. This causes problems for cheaters, as we shall see.

Both grudgers and suckers behave nicely towards everybody else, and both earn a high average payoff.

BUT...

In a population of mostly cheats a single grudger will not be successful, and will most likely go extinct. However, if the grudgers begin to grow in numbers, their chance of seeing and meeting each other becomes great enough *to off-set their wasted effort in grooming cheats.*

They can spend most of the time grooming each other, and the cheats will be driven out.

The cheats will never be driven to extinction (remember they have genes in other populations that are just as lucrative).

If we could nudge the cheats into becoming grudgers, like us the work that the cheaters are doing in those other populations may even turn out to be mutually beneficial. So, there's a chance for a grudging reconciliation somewhere down the line.

Cheat A is arguably the biggest AI research company in the world (even from its search product alone, although it has many others).

Every time a user does something with any one of its products, they are training the machines.

It can predict human intent better than anyone. And at the level of mass behaviour. Some of this research even flows back into the open-source world, already.

Cheat B is the greatest social experiment in the history of the human race. Again, operating at a mass level, discovering more about how people display traits, tastes, and skills to each other.

Winston Churchill was a bricklayer by trade— and a pretty tasty one by all accounts—but it still paid him to buy in that service from a professional bricklayer because he was an even better politician.

In Dawkins computer simulation he starts with a majority of suckers, a minority of grudgers that is just above the critical frequency, and about the same-sized minority of cheats.

'The first thing that happens is a dramatic crash in the population of suckers as the cheats ruthlessly exploit them.

But the cheats still have the grudgers to reckon with.

As the sucker population declines, the grudgers have also been getting a kicking from cheats, but are just about managing to bop their way back.

When the suckers are inevitably wiped out, that means the cheaters have no option but to change strategy, exploitation is not so easy when faced with a growing population of grudgers.

However, slowly and inexorably the cheats are driven out...and the grudgers are left in sole control.

It was the presence of suckers that actually held back the grudgers initially because they were easy fodder for the cheats.

Ultimately the cheats are almost out of the game, although a minority of will always hang around on the fringes. That's fine, though. It would keep grudgers on their toes, and prevent them from lapsing back into sucker ways.

Grudger turns out to be an evolutionarily stable strategy against cheat. An ESS is defined as a strategy which, *if most members of a population adopt it, cannot be bettered by an alternative strategy.*

Can you count, suckers? I say the future is ours... if you can count!

In the early 1960's Robert Axelrod, now a professor of political science at the University of Michigan was running computer simulations as part of an undergrad science project.

Inspired by news reports of the 1962 Cuban Missile Crisis - a 13-day stand-off between the USA and the Soviet Union after the discovery of Soviet missile stash in Cuba considered the nearest the Cold War came to escalating into a full-scale nuclear war - he set up a program to run *prisoner's dilemma* simulations, testing different strategies against each other.

He wondered if he could figure out a strategy for getting out of the arms race altogether. Was there a way for two or more parties with conflicting self-interests to cooperate, without either side getting *shafted* by the other.

Axelrod invited various professors to write a program that embodied their *strategy* and run them all against each other to find the winner.

Surprisingly the winning strategy was also the simplest – running to only two lines of code. The best strategy was called *tit for tat*.

Be nice first, then do whatever the other guy did on the last move.

Look for cooperation if there's any inclination, but if there's not, bear a *grudge*.

Devised by mathematical psychologist Anatol Rapaport, tit for tat involves cooperating with your partner on the first encounter, then adjusting your behaviour to match theirs (*do unto others whatever they just did unto you*).

As long as they cooperate, you continue to cooperate, but if they defect, you respond with retaliation against them. You ain't a sucker.

In the tournaments, any strictly selfish strategy couldn't beat it.

The genius of tit for tat lies in how it protects the individual against nasty opponents, never letting themselves to be exploited because of being too nice. A *sucker*.

It avoids the ongoing losses that would come from *mutual vengefulness* – stupidly sacrificing their self-interest just to get even. Cutting off one's nose to spite one's face.

It encourages fair play by rewarding others for cooperating while punishing them for defecting, all the time making its intent absolutely clear. It can be trusted by the other players.

In the 2011 movie *Limitless* a struggling writer, Eddie Morra, is accidentally introduced to NZT, a *cognitive overdrive drug* that gives him mental super-powers - akin to a superhuman AI.

Morra decides to *get on one* and turns in his

novel in a matter of days. Next, Eddie's attentions shift to matters of global finance and, such is his meteoric success in that field too, he quickly draws attention from ruthless business mogul Carl Van Loon (played by Robert DeNiro), who ropes him in as a principal advisor.

But soon Morra starts to be indiscreet, ostentatious and 'disrespects' his new powers, and the hard-nosed Van Loon cuts him down.

'Your deductive powers are a gift from God or chance or a straight shot of sperm or whatever or whoever wrote your life-script. A gift, not earned.

You do not know what I know because you have not earned those powers.

You're careless with those powers, you flaunt them, and you throw them around like a brat with his trust-fund. You haven't had to climb up all the greasy little rungs. You haven't been bored blind at the fundraisers.

You haven't done the time and that first marriage to the girl with the right father.

You think you can leap over all in a single bound.

You haven't had to bribe or charm or threat your way to a seat at that table.

You don't know how to assess your competition because you haven't competed.'

At least in part, the Mark Zuckerbergs of this world have risen to the top without having to compete. He's on record admitting as much.

'You don't get to be successful like this just by being hard-working or having a good idea. You have to get lucky.'

But paying your dues from the top is a better vantage point than from the bottom.

To be fair, Zuck was well aware of his limitations. That's why he brought in Sheryl Sandberg as COO.

Under Sandberg, targeted advertising became the company's new focus, and Facebook became a profitable business for the first time in 2010, growing into one of the most powerful companies in the world.

Sandberg rightly received the accolades.

She knew how to *compete.*

Educated at Harvard, watched over by her mentor Larry Summers at the World Bank before moving into the US Treasury Department, she really arrived on the scene when she jumped ship to Google and quickly honed its online advertising juggernaut.

In 2007 Zuck nicked Sandberg off his rivals with one simple instruction. Make Facebook profitable.

It took her just two years to turn that around. And in some style, too – last year Facebook pulled in $50 billion in advertising revenue – and depending on which stats you believe, share anything between 70%-90% of every dollar spent in digital advertising along with Google.

(That the whole online advertising debacle is a big mess is neither here nor there for the purposes of this argument. The big two have been better at figuring out how to make it work for them.)

Sandberg was the grown-up.

She had *climbed up all the greasy little*

rungs. She knew how to compete.

That's what she was there to do.

Certain publishers, The New York Times and The Guardian in particular, continually have their knickers in a twist over Sheryl.

When faced with growing criticism and pressure over its handling of the so-called fake news debacle, suspected election interference from the Russians, mishandling of user data and other misdemeanours – Sandberg set into play a strategy to suppress information about the issues, discredit its critics, and *deflect blame* onto its competitors, like Google. To do this, she employed several 'crisis PR' firms that specialise in these less than wholesome tactics.

Everything is PR.

When the House Financial Services Committee wanted to quiz Facebook over their cryptocurrency project, they insisted Zuck took the stand rather than Sheryl. Alexandria Ocasio-Cortez shifted the conversation quickly away from the subject to probing on Facebook's policies on speech and political ads on its platform.

The shifty Zuck made AOC look better than she was. If Sandberg had been allowed to do the gig, Ocasio-Cortez would have got short shrift.

Because this is precisely what Sandberg was hired by Facebook to do. Be the grown-up, grow the business, make it profitable.

Part and parcel of turning Zuck's *gift from God or chance or a straight shot of sperm* into corporate America would probably entail the occasional resort to one or two *cute* moves. This is how you compete.

The problem is that a lot of people believed Zuckerberg (a bit) and Sandberg (a lot) were something different.

They wanted them to be different. They saw them as part of the 'celebrity' or 'informal' CEO lineage, started by Branson and Jobs, the vanguard of the new era of 'neat' capitalism – that links consumption with personal *empowerment*.

(This idea probably reached its zenith - or nadir, depending on your point of view - with Sinek and *Start With Why*.)

For Sandberg, it's just been six years since published her own addition to the leadership canon. *Lean In: Women, Work, and the Will to Lead,* quickly became the manifesto of the mission to reboot feminism in the boardroom.

'Lean In...' perfectly captured the zeitgeist. Tacking all aspects of gender inequality in the global workplace, urging women to stop holding themselves back, to *lean in rather than leaning back.* It was inspirational stuff.

The book became a massive global bestseller, but its impact reached further launching a network and movement of 'Lean-In Communities' around the world with an enviable corporate sponsor list including P&G, Coca-Cola (and *ahem* Google). All of this has propelled Sandberg into arguably our biggest celebrity executive.

But was it all a sham?

Is this just corporate impression management?

Had all this bluster served only as another deceptive move designed only to ensure Sheryl's place in the TIME 100 list of the most influential people in the world? Moreover, does having more powerful women in powerful positions mean nothing if all they're doing is leaning into 'exploitative capitalist conventions'.

Was the whole *Lean In* deal advancing the cause of women's equality or was *Lean In* using women's equality to advance the cause of brand Sandberg? As with most (false) dichotomies, the truth is somewhere in between.

Is this why so many feel as if they have been cheated?

When dolphins were found to be attacking porpoises off the coast of Scotland, some 'experts' attributed this 'aberrant behaviour' to pollution, an assertion for which they admitted they had no evidence. They just didn't want 'nasty' dolphins to be real.

This is what Matt Ridley has labelled *eliminate the negative and sentimentalise the positive.*

Either way, deception – real or imagined – will induce anger and attack.

To illustrate, I love this story recounted by the legendary Robert Trivers in his book *Deceit and*

Self-Deception.

While taking a walk in Central Park with his then one-year-old son on his back, Trivers spotted a squirrel in a tree.

His son did not see the furry forest friend, so Trivers whistled to draw it closer, and sure enough, the squirrel crept forward on the branch.

But the boy still could not see it.

Trivers then switched strategy and mimicked an attack on the squirrel.

Lunging at it, he expected the creature to scarper and so allow his boy to see it.

'Instead, the squirrel ran straight at us, chittering in apparent rage, teeth fully exposed, jumping to the branch closest to me and my son. Now my son saw the squirrel, and I had the fright of my life, quickly running several steps away.

For my folly, the squirrel could have killed my son with a leap to my shoulders and two expert bites to his neck.

Had I begun the relationship hostile, I believe

the squirrel never would have become so angry. It was the betrayal implied by beginning friendly, only then to attack (deception) that triggered the enormous anger'.

If I had the dough and a business to build, Sheryl would be top of my call list.

She knows how to compete. She's got her boxing gloves on. And, like it or not, to really *lean in* means not always playing nice.

My sense is that the NYT and Sandberg's critics have failed to find the balance between their unhealthy naivety and a healthy dose of cynicism.

Business is business, and *idealised descriptions* are all well and good as window dressing, but should not be taken too seriously in practice.

* * *

The naturalistic fallacy, as outlined by Scottish Enlightenment philosopher David Hume, is the leap from *is to ought*.

The tendency to believe that what *is*, is good; therefore, what *is*, is what ought to be.

The moralistic fallacy is the opposite. It refers to

the leap from *ought* to *is*. To claim that the way things *should be* is the way they *are*.

Sometimes called the *reverse naturalistic fallacy*.

For example, take some randomly selected Simon Sinek platitude like this:

'Great companies don't hire skilled people and motivate them; they hire already motivated people and inspire them'.

Or how about:

'The goal is not to do business with everybody who needs what you have. The goal is to do business with people who believe what you believe.'

Nice ideas. But just because that's the way things ought to be doesn't mean it's anything like the way things are in the real world.

This kind of glibness falls squarely into the *reverse naturalistic* bucket, which makes them great fodder for the masses of Linkedin *suckers*.

Probably intelligent people.

Sadly, intelligence and rational thinking – although related - represent two fundamentally different constructs.

Some psychologists like the term 'dysrationalia' (we like that too, and we're pitching a pilot to Netflix).

The inability to reason despite having adequate intelligence.

And outside of Simon Sinek's world, for most people, the reality of their jobs is somewhat different. It is closer to what David Graeber, the anarchist philosopher, calls 'the shift towards an immaterial economy'. One that creates large numbers of jobs without any apparent social value and experienced as being purposeless and empty by their occupants.'

Although this does free up more time for activities better suited to these harsh environmental conditions and under high levels of competition. Social comparison and status-seeking, for example.

Sinek himself is no *sucker*, of course. I'd kill for one-tenth of his book sales.

The simple way for businesses to avoid the traps in both fallacies is by simply *never* talking about what *ought to be* and only talking about *what is*.

Avoid drawing moral conclusions and implications from observations and don't allow observations to be directed by any moral and political principles.

A reality check on human behaviour. If we understand this, then designing interventions is easier. The hard part is accepting what *is* being human.

Self-interest first, always.
Short-term focus
Obsession with status
Copying other people
Reacting to immediate sensory cues.

In Axelrod's final experiment, the only strategy that could improve on tit-for-tat was a slight variant of itself. One small tweak to the code that fully optimised the program. The second line of code, the one that says do whatever the other guy did last, is modified.

Don't *always* retaliate, but *nearly* always retaliate.

This became known as *generous tit for tat*.

Adopt a position of cooperation as long as the other side does, too. If the other lot begin to cheat, then we stop cooperating as well, to show that there are consequences for cheating. But the door stays *forgivingly* open to future cooperation, without being a *sucker*.

The precise and mutually beneficial strategy of generous tit for tat in the news media and big-tech-two scenario requires that both parties agree to never the first to defect, but be willing to defect (in retaliation). But be *forgiving* (willing to break a defection cycle), and be non-envious (do not specifically attempt to attack opponents).

In this way, an entity that is basically selfish can still relentlessly pursue their own self-interest simply by *deciding* to be nice—even if it's only a strategy. They don't even have to *mean* it!

And, *generously*, they can initiate renewed self-interested cooperation from time to time, to play nicely. But hanging on to a *grudge* all the same.

People funny, bwoy.

WE ARE HERE TO DO JUST WHAT YOU WANT US TO

Do you think that you could make it,
with Frankenstein?

THE FRANKENSTEIN COMPLEX IS a term coined by 20th-century American author and biochemistry professor Isaac Asimov in his famous *robot novels* series. Between 1939 and continuing almost right up to his death in 1992, Asimov produced nearly 40 short stories and six complete novels on the *robot* theme as well as numerous other *science fiction* and *science fact* books and essays.

'The Frankenstein complex' describes the feeling of fear we hold that our inventions will inevitably turn on us - their creators – like that of the monster in Mary Shelley's 1818 novel, arguably the first *science-fiction* novel.

Over two hundred years later we still seem worried about this idea of subordination – that we are losing the ability to 'control' our machines and becoming a world where technology controls people instead of us controlling technology.

That stories like *Frankenstein* capture the imagination doesn't mean that they are likely to come true in *the future*, but they often tell us something about the *present*.

The key lesson from Mary Shelley's tale is that when Victor Frankenstein gave life to his monster, he was so blinded by ambition that gave scant consideration to the moral consequences. There was no Jeff Goldblum around to tell him that *just because he could doesn't mean he should*.

Are we facing a similar moral dilemma? What are we unleashing with artificial intelligence?

With *robots*?

The word *robot* comes from an old Slavonic word *rabota*, which, roughly translated, means the *servitude of forced labour*. Rabota was the kind of work that serfs would have had to perform, on their masters' lands, in the Middle Ages.

Rabota was further adapted in the 1920s by the Czech playwright, sci-fi novelist and journalist Karel Capek, in the title of his controversial 1920 hit play, *R.U.R. Rossumovi Univerzální Roboti* (Rossum's Universal Robots).

In this futuristic drama (it's set in circa 2000) R.U.R. is a company who mass-produce robot 'workers' (slaves) using the latest biology, chemistry and technology.

These robots are not mechanical *devices*, but instead, they are artificial organisms – a bit like Kraftwerk's Showroom Dummies (or for younger readers, think of the 'hosts' in the Westworld HBO TV series) – and they are chiefly designed to perform all the work that humans would rather outsource.

We are programmed just to do...anything you want us to.

There was some considerable excitement in the Pritchard household when it was announced that Kraftwerk would be headlining the 2013 Vivid Festival at Sydney Opera House. Billed as 'The Catalogue', the 'Werk would perform eight shows over four days, each featuring one of their most iconic studio masterworks in full.

First *Autobahn* from 1974 and '75s *Radio-Activity*, then the big three; *Trans Europe Express*, *The Man-Machine* through to *Computer World* spanning 77-81, then finishing up with 1986's *Techno Pop*, followed by *The Mix* (a 'hits' remix project from '91) and finally *Tour de France* from 2003.

Unfamiliar with the lottery system employed in the ticketing of 'high demand' events, I decorously applied for all eight shows in the hope of securing seats for at least one.

I got the lot.

Despite being *au fait* with many of the FOMO behavioural tricks and nudges routinely applied by airline e-commerce sites and the like – and I've used these tricks myself on numerous occasions – I fell for it, like the *sucker* I am. Powerless to resist.

Where is a probabilistic, fuzzy-matching personal AI when you need one?

I am programmed just to do...anything you want me to.

In Capek's 1920s, it should be noted that we were a good 30 years off the modern concept of genetic engineering (DNA's role in heredity was not confirmed until 1952) and the robots themselves, while quasi-biological, are assembled factory-like, as opposed to grown or 'born'.

It turns out there's an almost infinite market for this service until, *naturellement*, the robots eventually conspire to take over the world. In the process of domination, the formula required to create new 'robots' has unfortunately been destroyed and - because the robots have killed everybody who knows how to make new robots - their own extinction looms.

But redemption is always at hand.

Consciousness spontaneously emerges in two robots, a 'male' and a 'female'; consequently, they develop the 'human abilities' to love and experience emotions, and – like an android Adam and Eve – set off together to make a new world.

At least part of the problem we have with this machine age is the concern about AI alignment.

Alignment is generally accepted as the ongoing challenge of ensuring that we produce AIs that are aligned with human values.

This is our modern Frankenstein complex.

For example, if a so-called AGI (Artificial 'General' Intelligence) ever did develop at some point in the future, would it do what we (humans) wanted it to do?

Would/could any SuperAI values 'align' with human values? The argument might be that AI can be said to be aligned with human values when it does what humans want, but...

Will AI do things some humans want, but that other humans don't want?

How will AI know what humans want given that we often do what we want but not what we 'need' to do? And what if t*he most terrifying thing is what people do want?*

And – given that it is a 'superintelligence' - what will AI do if these human values conflict with its values.

Of course, the notion that we'll make any AIs into a 'general-purpose intelligence', *like our own* is dubious.

Yes, the human mind is a computational system, but there is nothing particularly *general purpose* in its design. It's composed of many different specialised programs - evolved adaptations - and these adaptations evolved at various times over our evolutionary history.

These are distinct software modules – individual AIs - pre-programmed with knowledge about how to pursue particular goals, or how to acquire the knowledge needed. Each of these programs is 'designed' by natural selection to execute *its own* functions when it detects that a problem that it evolved to solve is at hand.

In this sense, we are *adaptation executors*.

We don't need any mythical AGI – just one mental module gone rogue could do some pretty serious damage.

In the notorious thought experiment AI pioneer

Eliezer Yudkowsky wonders if we can specifically prevent the creation of super-intelligent AIs like the *paperclip maximiser*.

In the paperclip maximiser scenario, a bunch of engineers are trying to work out an efficient way to manufacture paperclips, and they accidentally invent an artificial 'super' intelligence.

This AI is a relentless utility-maximising agent whose utility is a direct function of the number of paperclips it makes.

The engineers go home for the night, but by the time they've returned to the lab the next day, this AI has copied itself onto every computer on the planet and begun redeploying the world's resources to give itself more power to boost its intelligence.

Now, having control of all the computers and machines on earth, it proceeds to annihilate all life and disassembles the entire world into its constituent atoms to make as many paperclips as possible.

Presumably, this kind of scenario is what is troubling Elon Musk when he dramatically worries that '...with artificial intelligence, we are summoning the demon.'

Musk - when not supervising the assembly of his AI-powered self-driving cars can be found hanging out in his SpaceX data Centre's 'Cyberdyne Systems' (named after the fictitious company that created 'Skynet' in the Terminator movie series) - might have some covert agenda at play in expressing his AI fears given how deep rival tech giants Google and Facebook are in the space. Who knows?

But there seems to be some reasonableness to this fear. In *Enlightenment Now* the psychologist Steven Pinker expressed the logic in this way:

Since humans have more intelligence than animals - and AI robots of the future will have more of it than us – and we have used our powers to domesticate or exterminate less well-endowed animals (and more technologically advanced societies have enslaved or annihilated technologically primitive ones), it inevitably follows that any super-smart AI would do the same to us. And we will be powerless to stop it.

Except this scenario is highly unlikely, it

confuses intelligence with motivation.

Even if we did invent superhuman intelligent robots, why would they want to take over the world? Knowledge is acquired by formulating explanations and testing them against reality, not by running an algorithm and in any case, big data is still finite data, whereas the universe of knowledge is infinite.

What is true is that we are facing a near future where robots will indeed be our direct competitors in many workplaces.

As more and more employers put artificial intelligence to work, any position involving repetition or routine is at risk of extinction. In the short-term humans will almost certainly lose out on jobs like accounting and bank telling. Farm labourers, paralegals, pharmacists and media buyers are all in the same boat.

Any occupations that share a predictable pattern of repetitive activities, the likes of which are possible to replicate through Machine Learning algorithms, will almost certainly bite the dust.

We have dealt with the impact of technological

change on the world of work many times. Two hundred years ago, about 98 per cent of the US population worked in farming and agriculture, now it's about 2 per cent, and then the rise of factory automation during the early part of the 20th century — and the outsourcing of manufacturing to countries like China - has meant that there is much less need for labour in Western countries.

Indeed, much of Donald Trump's schtick around bringing manufacturing back to America from China is ultimately fallacious and uses China as a convenient scapegoat. Even if it were possible to make American manufacturing great again, because of the relentless rise of automation, any rejuvenated factories would only require a tiny fraction of human workers.

Even those banking on 'new economy' poster-children like Uber are realising that it's not a long game - autonomous car technology means that very shortly these drivers will be surplus to requirements.

In his huge-selling book 'Homo Deus' the historian Yuval Noah Harari speculates that in the same way that the industrial revolution of the 19th century created the 'working class', the AI revolution will create a new un-working class.

After all, what's the point of the masses once algorithms can do almost everything better than humans?

Harari's reasoning runs like this

For a start, organisms themselves are basically *algorithms*. An assemblage of organic algorithms shaped by natural selection over millions of years of evolution.

Algorithmic calculations are not affected by the materials from which the calculator is built. So there's no reason to think that organic algorithms can do things that non-organic algorithms can't potentially do just as well, or better.

Harari uses the example of facial recognition – something that babies can do almost from day one but even the most powerful computers struggled with until very recently. But within just a couple of years of that first breakthrough, the current facial-recognition technologies can identify people far faster and more efficiently and quickly than humans and are one of the cornerstones of the emerging surveillance economy.

Are we not men? We are Devo.
De-evolving?

It becomes easier to replace humans in many domains because the algorithms are getting smarter, and if we are becoming dumber.

The *law of irreversibility*, first stated in 1893 by the paleontologist Louis Dollo, scuppered the possibility of devolution *by demonstrating how improbable it was that evolution would follow the same path twice, albeit backwards.*

Harari suggests that humans are, however, professionalising ourselves into redundancy, at least.

It would be immensely difficult to design a robotic version of one of our Stone-age ancestors. They had to be competent in a wide variety of hunter-gatherer skills whereas the skills that the average modern human brings to modern jobs inhabit in a much narrower niche and would be much easier to replace. A new *unworking class* would be a useless class of people with no economic or political importance or value, who contribute nothing to society, unemployed and unemployable.

Harari suggests that this useless class will be completely expendable, not even cannon fodder, given that future wars will be fought by algorithms. A sub-species kept occupied with drugs and computer games.

Or perhaps there's another solution that might already be in play.

New jobs indeed emerge as new technologies emerge replacing the old ones, although the jury is out on the value of many of these jobs.

In 1930, John Maynard Keynes predicted that by the century's end, technology would have advanced sufficiently that people in western economies would work a 15-hour week. In technological terms, this is entirely possible. But it didn't happen - if anything we are working more.

In his 2013 essay *On the Phenomenon of Bullshit Jobs*, David Graeber, Professor of Anthropology at the London School of Economics, says that Keynes didn't factor into his prediction the massive rise of consumerism. 'Given the choice between fewer hours and more toys and pleasures, we've collectively chosen the latter.'

Graeber argues that to fill up the time and keep consumerism rolling, many jobs have had to be created that are pointless. Rather than creating a massive reduction of working hours to free the world's population to pursue their own meaningful activities (as Keynes imagined), or the drugs and computer games route suggested by Harari, we have seen the creation of huge new administration industries without any apparent social value. And 'jobs' often experienced as being purposeless and empty by workers.

In our society, there seems a general rule that the more obviously one's work benefits other people; the less one is likely to be paid for it.

Even more perverse, there seems to be a broad sense that this is the way things should be.

When tabloids stir up resentment against tube workers for 'paralysing' London during contract disputes: the very fact that tube workers can bring London to a halt shows that their work is actually necessary, but this seems to be precisely what annoys people.

To be fair, robots are unrivalled at solving problems of rote learning, and humans struggle at this. But robot ability to understand human behaviour and make inferences about how the world works are still pretty limited.

Robots, AIs and algorithms can be said to 'know' things because their byte-addressable memories contain information. However, there is no evidence to suggest that we are close to any situation in which they *know they know* these things, or that they can reflect on their states of 'mind'.

They are *zero-order* intentional machines.

Intentionality is the term used by philosophers to refer to the state of having a state of mind – the ability to experience things like knowing, believing, thinking, wanting and understanding.

Think about it this way, third-order intentionality is required for even the simplest of human exchanges (where someone communicates to someone else that someone else did something). Then four levels are required to elevate this to the level of narrative ('the writer wants the reader to believe that character A thinks that character B intends to do something').

Most mammals (almost certainly all primates) are capable of reflecting on their state of mind, at least in a basic way - they know that they know. This is first-order intentional.

Humans rarely engage in more than fourth-order intentionality in daily life, and only the smartest can operate at sixth-order without getting into a tangle. (*Person 1 knows that Person 2 believes that Person 3 thinks that Person 4 wants Person 5 to suppose that Person 6 intends to do something*).

The next big leap for AIs would be with the acquisition first or second-order intentionality – only then the robots might just about start to understand that they are not human. The good news is that for the rest of this century we're probably safe enough from suffering any robot apocalypse.

The kind of roles requiring intellectual capital, creativity, human understanding and applied third/fourth level intentionality is always going to be crucial. And hairdressers.

And so, the viability of 'creative industries' like entertainment, media, and advertising, holds firm for the time being. No algorithm is likely to replicate intellectual capital, moral understanding and intentionality any time soon.

In the advertising and marketing business, it should be stating the obvious that we should compete largely on the strengths of our capability in those areas, but take a look inside the operations of many agencies and despair at how few of their people are spending time on critical thinking tasks and creativity.

Even more disappointing is when we'd rather debate whether creativity can be 'learned' by a robot rather than focusing on speeding up the automation of mundane activities.

Human and artificial intelligence should complement each other.

The AI revolution need not be our modern Frankenstein complex. Instead, it's the big opportunity to start over, to give us another bite at the Keynes cherry. Liberated to be more creative and put to use our miraculous innate abilities for empathy, for intentionality and high-level abstract reasoning, *augmented* by the *robots.*

The metaphor that often conflates human and machine learning is the idea of a *neural network.*

But the big difference between a human brain and an artificial neural network is the sheer scale of the brain's neural network in comparison. There are billions of neurons in the human brain and a gazillion connections between them.

It is because AI systems are so much simpler than the human brain that they can deal with far greater computational complexity in specific areas than humans can. Yes, it can process *particular data* at an incredible scale; but it isn't able to process information in the *multidimensional* way that human brains do.

In fact, it's the human ability to 'create' problems that makes us so good at solving them.

This factor is one of the distinctions between us and other primates. No-one would suggest that chimpanzees possess higher 'intelligence' than humans; however, they do seem to perform 'cognitively' better in specific domains.

The Cognitive trade-off hypothesis as proposed by primatologist Tetsuro Matsuzawa, suggests that losing short term memory was *one of the costs of our entering a new environment, the savannah, with different challenges than were faced by chimpanzees, who stayed in the forest.*

The hypothesis says that our language facility was developed at the cost of short-term memory, and that language (and the symbolic thinking that accompanies it) were more valuable to us than memory.

In Rebooting AI, authors Gary Marcus and Ernest Davies offer that the principal reason why people will overestimate what AI can actually achieve is that media reports overstate AI's abilities *as if every modest advance represents a paradigm shift.*

They also provide readers with a cheat sheet of six key questions to ask upon reading some sensational AI hyperbole:

1. *Strip away the rhetoric, ask what did the AI system actually do here?*

2. *How general is the result? (does an alleged [x] task measure all aspects of [x], or just a tiny piece of it?)*

3. *Is there a demo where I can try out my own examples? (Be sceptical if there isn't.)*

4. *If the proponents allege that an AI system is better than humans, then which humans, and how much better?*

5. *How far does succeeding at the particular task reported in the new research actually take us toward building genuine AI?*

6. *How robust is the system? Could it work just as well with other data sets, without massive amounts of retraining?*

(To be fair the scepticism the authors suggest is worth applying to market research of any sort...)

Wir sind auf alles programmiert,
Und was du willst wird ausgeführt

.

A MAN ON THE MAIN MOTOR MILE MESMERISED MUCH MONKEY MAGIC

It was just like,
Nothing on earth.

MAGICAL THINKING CAN BE SIMPLY described as the assigning of patterns and causation to events where those patterns and causation don't actually exist.

One of the explanations psychologists offer for why people engage in magical thinking is that it can help to give a sense of security – a feeling that one possesses some special knowledge about how to influence outcomes that would usually be out of one's control.

Sometimes it's just a bit of fun, of course.

The philosopher Daniel Dennett has this anecdote about his friend the theologian Lee Siegel.

Siegel, a professor of religion at the University of Hawaii, and an enthusiastic amateur magician has published many articles and books examining Indian religion and culture including a book on Indian street magic, *Net of Magic: Wonders and Deceptions in India*, published in 1991.

For him, India was a 'cauldron of illusions', where truth transcends mere fact, where these illusions serve as 'escapes from the discomforts' of life.

Reports that his next study is to be conducted in the insights team within a major marketing organisation remain unconfirmed.

Siegel explains that when he told friends and associates that he was writing a book on magic, he was often asked: 'Is it a book about real magic?'

By 'real magic' of course, people mean 'miracles' and acts involving 'supernatural powers'.

Seigel would answer, 'No, the book is about conjuring tricks, rope tricks, snake charming, illusions etc. Not real magic.'

So, when people say 'real magic', that really refers to the kind of magic that is *not real*.

The magic that cannot be done.

While the magic that *is real* - the kind of magic that CAN actually be done - is not 'real magic', it's a trick.

'Real magic' then, would need to be miraculous, or as Hume would have called it; a violation or transgression of the laws of nature.

 David Hume was one of the great philosophers of the 18th century Scottish Enlightenment.

This period in Scotland was characterised by a massive number of intellectual and scientific accomplishments and basically the invention of the modern world.

Even the French philosopher Voltaire once remarked that 'we look to Scotland for all our ideas of civilisation.'

Voltaire - a *nom de plume*, he was François-Marie to his *bons amis* – enjoyed a bit of *la comédie*, famously exhibiting his disdain for

Christianity by stating 'I have only ever made one prayer to God, a very short one: 'O Lord, make my enemies ridiculous.' And God granted it.'

(*Le temps passe*, Scotland can't even qualify for a World Cup these days, and French philosophy abandoned the Enlightenment, and *raison*, sometime in the late 20th century...)

Hume is best known today for his philosophical 'system' that combined empiricism, scepticism, and naturalism and had little time for notions of *real magic*.

Walking on water, turning water into wine, or *sending tweets through the power of thought* alone – to be fair, the latter is probably not that far off becoming the kind of magic that *can* be done - would be good examples of flying in the face of laws of nature.

Occurrences like that would be very troubling to science *if* they ever actually happened.

No testimony is sufficient to establish a miracle, unless the testimony be of such a kind, that its falsehood would be more miraculous than the fact which it endeavours to establish.

Suppose some *Thinkfluencepreneur* makes a claim that 'next year will see an acceleration in the trend towards marketers using influencers to create branded content, instead of agencies, production companies, and publishers.'

No matter how nice and trustworthy this individual might seem, the idea of he/she is just making shit up (or having an *aberrant salience psychosis episode*) would be less of a miracle than marketers binning agencies and publishers, wholesale, in favour of some spotty teenagers armed with iPhones and Instagram.

It's now just over 100 years since the famous Cottingley fairy hoax. Two spotty teenage English cousins called Frances Griffiths and Elsie Wright took photographs of 'fairies 'at the bottom of the garden of the house belonging to Elsie's parents in Cottingley, a leafy West Yorkshire village close to Bradford.

Of course, the photographs are clearly staged. The fairies are paper cut-outs Elsie had copied from a popular children's book, Princess Mary's Gift Book, published just a couple of years earlier in

1915. The girls were having a bit of creative fun, hoping to wind up Elsie's father, from whom they had borrowed the camera and been given some quick photography lessons.

It was all harmless fun until Elsie's mother, Polly, attended a lecture on 'spiritualism' a couple of years later. Following the talk, she dug out the photos bringing them to the attention of Edward Gardner, a leader of the Theosophical movement and the *Simon Sinek* of early 20th century England.

Boom! The photos were declared totally *'genuine unfaked photographs of a single exposure, open-air work, showing movement in all the fairy figures, and there is no trace whatever of studio work involving card or paper models, dark backgrounds or painted figures'.*

Very soon the validated fairy pictures began circulating throughout the spiritualist community and landed on the desk of Arthur Conan Doyle, creator of Sherlock Holmes.

While the fictional Holmes is arguably the epitome of rationality and scepticism, the avid spiritualist Doyle immediately endorsed the fairy pics as clear proof of the existence of supernatural entities.

Before you can say *'Once you eliminate the impossible, whatever remains, no matter how improbable, must be the truth'*, Doyle had sent Gardner up to West Yorkshire to interview the girls, collect some new photos of the fairies (and a couple of Gnomes who happened along), and penned an ecstatic article for the December 1920 issue of The Strand Magazine. Within weeks the Cottingley fairies became among the most widely recognised examples of early amateur photography in the world, their authenticity further endorsed by Gardner who - having taken a registered psychic with him on the trip *oop t'north*, just to be sure - declared the whole area to be teeming with fairies.

Things had clearly got out of hand, but the girls decided to roll with it. What started out as a bit of kid fun had seemingly caused a large group of adults to lose control of their minds completely. What should they do? Confess to the hoax and face the wrath of cheated believers? Or carry on with the fiction and go along with what the grown-ups want?

The thing is, the time was just about right in 1920 for the Cottingley fairies.

Throughout World War I, spiritualism had grown in popularity with the grieving British public. Amid the chaos of war, with deaths occurring in almost every family, there arose a sudden and concentrated interest in ideas of the afterlife. The prospect of being able to access some supernatural power, or otherworldly influence, would have been consoling.

Spiritualism, mediums and psychics role was twofold; to reunite families with their dead sons and husbands with 'evidence' that they were in a better place and as a reassurance of an afterlife that represented a promise of respite from the hardship and turmoil experienced during and after the Great War.

Of course, Spiritualism's success was its *entrepreneurial egalitarianism.*

The ability to incorporate a variety of other supernatural concepts, including fairies and gnomes, into its repertoire without blinking is phenomenal *agility.*

New technology also played a significant role. Arthur C. Clarke's Third Law states that any sufficiently advanced technology is *indistinguishable from magic.*

This was certainly the case in the early 20th century with the advent of 'radio', and telegraphy linking people together during the war. This was close to magical and gave people a way of understanding Spiritualism.

A medium making contact with the spirit world would 'tune-in' to the 'channels and wavelengths' of the 'other side'. Even the real world of wireless communications led to experiments in 'psychic telegraphs', which inventors claimed could pick up 'auras'. In 1920 even any kind of photography was still quite a new idea for ordinary people. The world's first mass-market camera, the Brownie from Eastman Kodak had only been invented twenty years earlier in 1900.

The most remarkable part of the Cottingley hoax is not that two young girls pretended they found fairies at the bottom of the garden. That is what children do. Play make-believe.

What is remarkable is that so many adults really wanted it to be true.

Fairies *and* gnomes.

Hume would have said that the chances that the girls, no matter how well-brought-up, were making it all up would still be a *smaller* miracle than the fairies actually existing. He encourages us to think about a miracle as an improbable event – an event whose improbability can be estimated on a kind of scale, and compared with an alternative such as fibbing.

A strange compulsion to believe in 'real magic' affects many people when the topic is advertising and brands.

This magical thinking assigns patterns and causation to events where patterns and causation do not exist.

When Clarke said indistinguishable from magic' did he mean 'real magic'? Or the kind of magic that *can* be done?

My good friend Mark Earls once proposed that we should try substituting the word 'Magic' for 'Big' in Big Data. 'If we only master *Magic Data*, it will make us all-powerful; the sword of *Magic Data* will banish all evils.'

Magic data is now inexorably linked to *magic* AI and *magical* machine learning. Lacking control increases something called illusory pattern recognition. That is, when individuals are induced to feel a lack of control, they tend to see meaningful patterns in random data, as if responding to their unfortunate lack of control by generating (false) coherence in data that would then give them greater control. Better data is what is needed.

Magical thinking is really about anxiety reduction. This also explains the enduring popularity of other 'magical' things like content marketing, influencers, the enduring cult of 'Lovemarks', and a multitude of other maladies.

Howard Gossage's observations back in the early 60s seem strangely prophetic, today.

'Advertising...is constantly being lured into seemingly allied fields that have little to do with its unique talents and often interfere with them. But there is one job it does well that no other

communication form does at all: the controlled propagation of an idea with defined objectives.'

This is a kind of magic that CAN be done - namely, make something creative and exciting and do whatever it takes to ensure people will see it.

It might not be 'real magic' but, when it works, it's magic nonetheless.

KJAFTAFOG

If you ever get close to a human
And human behaviour
Be ready, be ready to get confused

IT WASN'T THAT LONG AGO when the subject
matter and context in pop songs had somewhat
more substance and sense of enquiry.

Yes, kids, this was pop, believe it or not.

There's definitely, definitely,
no logic, to human behaviour
But yet so, yet so irresistible
And there is no map

Human Behaviour is the opening track on
Debut, the breakthrough album by Icelandic singer-
songwriter Björk. The set was produced by Bristol
Underground graduate Nellee Hooper and first
dropped in 1993.

Talking about the inspiration for the record, Björk looked back on her schooldays.

'When I went into the sixth form at school, I choose science, math and physics and thought psychology, anthropology, sociology and history and such was for sissies.

A huge majority of Icelanders do the same thing. They call subjects in school about people 'kjaftafog', which means *nattersubjects.*

As I got older and became a grown-up myself, I have learned to appreciate nattersubjects and recently read many books for the first time about psychology and... so I have learned a little about humans.'

But yet so, yet so irresistible
And there is no map

Is there a map? What does motivate human behaviour?

I've been a proponent of applied behavioural economics and suchlike in recent years, however, even invoking cognitive biases has now taken on 'magical' properties.

I had to sit on a panel for a client recently to help them evaluate creative pitches from a selection of top creative agencies.

I didn't have a vote I was just there to check that whatever was proposed was do-able from a media standpoint. For the most part, everything on show was *dreadfully* do-able.

Whether it was sensible to do these things is another question, although one that I was not required to answer.

Of course, I paid most attention to the strategy parts of the pitches. It's always interesting to see what the competition are up to, or where their heads are at.

Some form of applied pseudo-behavioural economics theory is clearly the *flavor du jour*.

It's been a remarkable rise. In just a few years behavioural economics has gained significant traction in advertising agencies to the point that nearly every planner and their dog now like to point out how human decision making has become bamboozled by biases.

The irony, of course, is that the standard line trotted out to preface the 'insights' – humans are irrational and make emotional decisions etc. – is as fallacious an example of thinking, as the thinking 'errors' of consumers the planner is trying to describe.

Similarly, the prevalent misconception (to be fair, I held this belief too, until recently) is that these cognitive biases 'produce' or 'cause' behaviour, when all they do is describe behaviour that's already happened. Planners fail to understand that biases are just tendencies and are also highly context-dependent.

This - very thin - focus on biases is unhelpful in several ways. It's *Wikipedia planning*.

 So much *kjaftafog*.

In those creative pitches I sat in on, every agency played a (magical) *loss aversion* card in their 'consumer insights' slide. Yet demonstrated little real understanding of the concept and where it might or might not come into play, and what purpose it serves in decision making.

They knew the 'name' of the thing, though.

To illustrate this point, there's a splendid anecdote from the great theoretical physicist – and erstwhile amateur safecracker/jazz bongo drummer Richard Feynman. His colleague and fellow physicist Murray Gell-Mann would complain that Feynman 'spent a great deal of time and energy generating anecdotes about himself'.

Many of these anecdotes are assembled in a couple of volumes, *Surely You're Joking, Mr Feynman!* and *What Do You Care What Other People Think?*

This one is from the latter, in which Feynman recalls holidays as a boy, spent in the Catskill Mountains, where many kids from New York City would go in the summer.

'On weekends, my father would take me for walks in the woods, and he'd tell me about interesting things that were going on. When the other mothers saw this...they wanted my father to take all the kids, but he didn't want to because he had a special relationship with me. So it ended up that the other fathers had to take their children for walks the next weekend.

The next Monday, when the fathers were all back at work, we kids were playing in a field. One kid says to me, 'See that bird? What kind of bird is that?'

I said, 'I haven't the slightest idea what kind of a bird it is.'

He says, 'It's a brown-throated thrush. Your father doesn't teach you anything!'

But it was the opposite.
He had already taught me.

'See that bird?' he said. 'It's a Spencer's warbler.' (He made that up. I knew he didn't know the real name.) 'Well, in Italian, it's a Chutto Lapittida. In Portuguese, it's a Bom da Peida. In Chinese, it's a Chung-long-tah, and in Japanese, it's a Katano Tekeda. You can know the name of that bird in all the languages of the world, but when you're finished, you'll know absolutely nothing whatever about the bird. You'll only know about humans in different places, and what they call the bird. So, let's look at the bird and see what it's doing—that's what counts.'

(I learned very early the difference between knowing the name of something and knowing something).

The thing is, most of these commonly invoked 'irrational' biases evolved for excellent, rational and adaptive reasons.

Leda Cosmides and John Tooby, the pioneers of evolutionary psychology, go so far as to say that '...despite widespread claims to the contrary, the human mind is not worse than rational...but may often be *better* than rational.'

When resources are scarce—as they were for 99.9% of our existence as a species—loss aversion would have been a perfectly rational bias to possess.

For early humans, the implications of losing a supply of food would have been significant.

Almost certain death.

Whereas gaining a week's worth of food meant survival and perhaps trade opportunities for one more week.

Another important concept in evolutionary

psychology is the mismatch theory. Evolutionary mismatch happens when the environment that we (or any organisms) have adapted to, over thousands of generations via the slow process of biological evolution, changes so quickly and intensely that certain behaviours or ways of thinking suddenly become potentially maladaptive in the new environment.

A simple description of mismatch theory is this.

If you have two options, Option A and Option B, and take option B when option A would be the adaptive choice, then a mismatch has occurred.

It is often said that the internet has been the great democratiser. Available to (just about) everyone and (just about) entirely directed by what people want. But the internet loves mismatch.

The most terrifying thing is just that. What people *do* want! Its a mismatch.

That adage was modified from an old quote from 60s theatre critic Clive Barnes (he was talking about TV). I can't find the original, but that one is close.

The advertisers' dilemma?

Should we be more concerned with *making things people want* rather than *making people want things*. But did advertising ever really *make* people *want* things?

Can it create 'emotional connections?'

Ad-people get terribly confused about is this thing called 'emotion'.

For a start, it's not just one thing.

There are distinctions between the functional emotion ('the emotional state'), the experience of the emotion and our ability to perceive and attribute emotions to other people (and to animals). Also, our ability to think and talk about emotion and - of particular interest to advertisers - the behaviours caused by an emotional state; the expressions and emotional responses.

But emotions are first and foremost about the states, and everything else flows from that.

In essence, to understand what emotions are, and what they are for, requires a fundamental or *ultimate* explanation.

When you're walking on the streets at night
Turn around and die of fright
What's that in the shadows?

Is it a dog?
Is it a cat?
Is it a dog?
What do you think of that?

The situation- detector circuit has perceived cues that indicate the possible presence of a threat.

The emotion state is fear.

Goals and motivational weightings change: Safety becomes a far higher priority.

Your entire focus narrows to the here and now, all information-gathering systems redirect towards the mission-critical. Is there someone about who can help me? Can I hide somewhere?

What's that in the shadows?

Your mind is a collection of evolved, *domain-specific* programs and whatever you are thinking and doing right now depends on which of these programs is currently in command of the ship.

It's not always neat. In fact, it's a bit messy.

Not least because these programs, or modules, all evolved at different times in our evolutionary history. Not only that, they are quite distinct from one another, and can (simultaneously) hold contradictory views.

Although, I'm in two minds about that.

Each of these programs is functionally specialised for solving a different *adaptive* problem that arose in what is called the *Environment of Evolutionary Adaptedness*, or EEA.

EEA describes the situational and external factors in which an evolved trait adapted over time. And the collective influence of selection pressures that caused an adaptation to develop.

The EEA of early humans that produced our brain development – from around one million years ago until around ten thousand years ago - is very different from our modern world.

Our brains and minds evolved to operate in hunter-gatherer and nomadic societies.

And so, it's an important distinction to make. Being well adapted to a particular environment and being *adaptable to environmental change* are different.

This is why many psychologists are arguing that many of the problems we face in the modern world are down to modern society representing this evolutionary *'mismatch'*.

As we touched on earlier, mismatch happens when people (or a species) are faced with a fast-changing environment to which their bodies and minds – their hardware and software – are not well-adapted.

We should be afraid of cars and electricity. But we're not. These are *evolutionarily novel* sources of danger. Too novel for our old equipment. Instead, our innate fears - spiders, snakes and the dark - have more ancient origins.

Another ancient fear is social exclusion; after all, expulsion from the tribe would have meant almost certain death.

(I have so many LinkedIn connections...but why don't they share my post?)

Each of these mental modules, our software

or *apps*, is a specialised structure sculpted to carry out a particular function. But integrated into a complex whole, and activated by a different set of cues.

These functions include basic things like breathing, heart-rate regulation, sleep management, and perception.

Alongside all-important social mechanisms; designed for face recognition, mate choice and 'reading' other peoples' minds. A more 'recent' adaptation is language, of course.

Steven Pinker describes resulting social behaviour as the outcome of *an internal struggle among many mental modules*, and it is *played out on the chessboard of opportunities and constraints defined by other people's behaviour.*

Of course, this internal struggle between cognitive programs creates another adaptive problem.

Programs that are designed to solve very specific adaptive problems could, if activated at the same time, conflict with one another, interfering with each other.

For instance, a sleep mechanism has to be over-ridden if cues for self-protection are present. If the house is on fire, you better get out.

To avoid misfires, the mind must then be equipped with what Tooby and Cosmides call *superordinate programs* that can override some programs when others are activated.

At the same time, some adaptive issues are best solved by activation of multiple mechanisms concurrently, running from the fire in the dark needs to pump up heart rate regulation and spatial awareness mechanisms.

A superordinate system is needed to co-ordinate the activity of neural systems, *snapping each into the right configuration at the right time.* Emotions are functional states that regulate behaviours.

This is what Emotions are *for.*

They orchestrate the mind's many and varied subprograms so that at any given time the organism is functionally coordinated.

Emotions are adaptations that have arisen in response to the adaptive problem of mechanism orchestration - Tooby & Cosmides.

Emotions arose and assumed their structures in response to conditions, contingencies, situations, or types of events that recurred during evolutionary history.

Avoiding and escaping from predators, parenting, exchange of trade and favours, establishing rank and status, dealing with the death of family members. Anger, revenge and love. Deciding what to eat (and not) and predicting other peoples' behaviour. These are just a few.

Repeated encounters with these situations selected for adaptations that guided information-processing and behaviour.

Emotions are the superordinate programs that mobilise a subset of the mental mechanisms in any given configuration in response to recurrent situations.

When a condition or situation of *an evolutionarily recognisable kind is detected*, a signal goes out from the emotion radar that activates the specific combination of subprograms appropriate to solving that type of adaptive problem(s) - and also deactivates programs whose operation might interfere with solving the most pressing issue.

In 'simple' terms, an emotion is a SUPERORDINATE program whose function is to direct the activities and interactions of the other mental subprograms.

> *Perception; attention; inference; learning; memory; goal choice; motivational priorities; categorisation and conceptual frameworks; physiological reactions; reflexes; behavioural decision rules; motor systems; communication processes; energy level and effort allocation; affective colouration of events and stimuli; recalibration of probability estimates, situation assessments, values, self-esteem, estimations of relative formidability, relative value of alternative goal states, and so on.*

Because emotions are clearly a product of adaptive design, they cannot be irrational. In fact, emotions are super-rational adaptations, finely tuned to countering threats and recognising opportunities.

An emotion cannot be reduced down to any one *category of effects* because it contains evolved instructions for ALL OF THEM.

Reducing the assessment of advertising to 'emotional' or 'rational' appeals or entertaining 'new data' that claims to compare the *emotional connection* rankings of top brands is nonsensical.

There's either a *response* or *no response*. Your superordinate system of emotions will decide.

The Dutch ethologist and ornithologist, Nikolaas Tinbergen - along with colleagues Karl von Frisch and Konrad Lorenz - received the 1973 Nobel Prize in Physiology and Medicine for their 'discoveries concerning organisation and elicitation of individual and social behaviour patterns'.

Alongside this accolade, Tinbergen's most famous contribution to science is the 'four questions' framework, posed initially in his 1963 article *'On Aims and Methods of Ethology'*.

This simple framework goes a long way towards explaining how and why any animal exhibits a behaviour and was instrumental in putting the nature vs nurture debate to bed once and for all.

The model shows how all behaviour (and all traits) are products of complicated interactions between genes and the environment.

Tinbergen and his colleagues argued that any analysis must address four aspects of a trait.

How it works, what function it serves, how it develops, and its evolutionary history.

Not explicitly *evolutionary,* Tinbergen's Four Questions - as they have since come to be known – detail the primary considerations a researcher should want to make, nevertheless. And they still hold.

(Ethologists tended to focus on observable behaviour and so didn't go deep into the psychological mechanisms, that came later as areas of ethology morphed into evolutionary psychology.)

The four questions are grouped under two headings.

Firstly, *Proximate* questions.

What are the mechanisms? - how does the behaviour get elicited, what signals or primes are required, and which pathways within the organism are involved?

How does it develop? - how does the behaviour change with age, experience and environment?

Ultimate questions.

Why did it evolve? - how did evolution and earlier generations/species contribute to this particular behaviour? Why did this behaviour help the organism/species survive/reproduce?

To illustrate how this framework can be applied, think of the last time you stuffed a Big Mac into your face. What was the decision process behind that? Was I hungry? Perhaps it was just convenient? I had a hangover? Or it's a treat now and again?

These kinds of explanations for behaviour operate at the proximate level.

These causes point to relatively up-close and immediately present influences—to what you are presently feeling or thinking or a plausible story you tell yourself.

Yes, proximate reasons are important, but they tell only tell part of the story.

Proximate reasons don't address the broader question of why Big Macs are appealing in the first place. Understanding the deeper reasons for preferences and behaviour requires an ultimate explanation. Ultimate explanations focus not on the relatively immediate triggers of behaviour, but on its evolutionary function.

In the Big Mac scenario, humans have psychological mechanisms that respond positively to the sight, smell, and taste of foods rich in sugars and fats.

These mechanisms exist because an attraction to these kinds of foods helped our ancestors obtain calories and survive in an environment where they were often scarce.

So, whereas the proximate reasons you bought a Big Mac may be many and varied, the ultimate cause is that a desire for sugary and fatty foods helped solve the critical evolutionary challenge of survival in the ancestral environment.

McDonald's, Burger King and KFC have become some of the biggest brands in the world and splash colossal global advertising budgets. However, it's no accident that they got there selling burgers, fried chicken and milkshakes rather than salad.

Market researchers, like social scientists, have typically been concerned with the proximate influences on behaviour.

However, an evolutionary perspective highlights that there is a deeper level of explanation rooted in the adaptive function of behaviour.

This is a useful lens through which to look at motivation because while there could be any amount of proximate motives for a given behaviour and many goals people pursue, there is a much smaller set of ultimate evolutionary functions that behaviour might serve.

These functions are rooted deep in our long evolutionary history; they shape all stages of consumer journeys and decision-making processes.

From the consumer brands we buy to the political brands we vote for.

Science is what it is and, as the saying goes, the universe is under no obligation to make sense to you. No moral sense, anyway.

When Cambridge Analytica - the technology consulting firm that worked for the 'Leave' lobby on *Brexit* and the 2016 Trump US election effort - obtained Facebook user data to create psychographic profiles of voters they then employed 'microtargeting' tactics to deliver specific messages that would resonate with those particular voters.

Legend has it that by examining just 150 'likes', their model could profile an individual user's *personality traits* with almost pinpoint accuracy.

It's been claimed that this use of personality 'profiling' and psychometric techniques amounted to 'weapons of psychological warfare' (sic) and generating a minor moral panic around established science simply because of the application by bad actors.

Just because we might not agree with the methods and aims of their campaign does not invalidate the science. All marketers should know that psychometrics have a much greater predictive power for behaviour than demographics or other segmentation types typically used in advertising.

What CA and the other actors in the Facebook data debacle attempted to do with data in combination with the other elements of *skullduggery* reported should be rightly frowned upon.

But this does not invalidate the science.

For ad people unfamiliar with the Big 5 personality traits model, perhaps the most useful summary - for our purposes - is in '*Spent*', an evolutionary perspective on consumer behaviour by the psychologist Geoffrey Miller.

Most readers will understand the distribution of human intelligence. It forms a bell curve, with most people clustered around the middle, close to IQ 100 – the average. Distribution tapers off relatively quickly as scores deviate so that *blockheads* and *geniuses* are rare. All the Big Five personality traits follow a similar bell-curve distribution.

Most people sit near the middle of the curve on the other traits, openness, conscientiousness, agreeableness, emotional stability and introversion/extraversion, either slightly lower or higher.

The Big 5 (plus IQ) is established science whereas the typical demographic/personality types used in market segmentation studies, for example, are mostly complete fiction.

When sex/gender, birthplace, language, cultural background, economic status, and education appear to predict consumer behaviour, the real reason is that these factors correlate with the Big 5 + IQ traits, not because they directly cause the behaviour.

Similarly, the commonly used organisational 'personality' frameworks like Myers-Briggs and HBDI are also nonsensical – because traits are normally distributed. Next time you hear a management guru talk about 'emotional intelligence' kick them in the eye.

Importantly, the big five traits can predict social, political, and religious attitudes reasonably well and can, therefore, be used to nudge people to act in line with their make-up (and corresponding moral foundations).

Left-leaning people tend to show higher openness (more interest in diversity), lower conscientiousness (less bothered with convention), and higher agreeableness (concern for care and fairness).

Conservatives show lower openness (more traditionalism), higher conscientiousness (family-values, sense of duty), and lower agreeableness (self-interests and nationalism, etc.).

That's one data point. These methods can be used by bad actors for nefarious means or slightly less bad actors for advertising means.

But the science is what it is.

These universal traits are relatively independent and don't correlate particularly; people display all six characteristics in different ways and combinations.

Although intelligent people tend to be more open than average to new experiences, there are plenty of smart people, who stick to their football, reality TV and the pub.

Likewise, there are plenty of open-minded people who love strange ideas and experiences, but who are not very smart. This explains the market for dubious new technology products and *alternative* wellness products like homoeopathy. Open-minded but not so intelligent can equal gullible.

For ad types, much of the research suggests that short-term creative intelligence is basically general intelligence plus openness. At the same time, long-term creative achievement is also predicted by higher than average conscientiousness and extraversion traits.

Account people could get by on middling for most traits, but above average emotional stability is a must-have. Planners would need to score reasonably high on both intelligence and trait conscientiousness but are more likely to be disagreeable.

To be a good planner, possession of a *quiet* disagreeableness is mandatory but also required is the ability to *fake agreeableness* out in the open. I've never got the hang of that.

So much *kjaftafog*.

THEY MUST HAVE COME TO A SECRET UNDERSTANDING

I don't deal in messages,
I deal in ideas and the effects of ideas.

MAGAZINE WERE A BIT TOO prog for punk, but too punky for the Bowie/Eno art-rock crowd. They were critically acclaimed by the more cerebral end of the music press, but the records didn't trouble the charts.

Their new-wavey art sound—although heavily-influenced by Bowie's *Low* era —sounded like nothing else when their first album, *Real Life*, dropped in 1978.

And Howard Devoto's bleak *existentialist* lyrics - preoccupied with death, madness, paranoia and alienation - were never going to be top 40 fodder.

In fact, *Real Life* sounds more like something from the early Roxy Music canon than anything else in punk at the time.

But nothing approaching Roxy-esque commercial success ever came, and outside of the, *possibly too- clever-for-its-own-good*, post-punk intelligentsia the legacy of Magazine remains in the margins.

In February 1977, Devoto had quit Buzzcocks (no 'the' please), the band he'd co-founded only a few months earlier with fellow Bolton Institute of Technology student, Pete Shelley.

This remarkable act of seemingly self-sabotage came just days after of the release of the band's first document, the *Spiral Scratch* EP. The EP was released on 29th January 1977 on the band's own New Hormones label, making Buzzcocks the first British punk group to establish an independent record label.

Simon Reynolds, in his book covering the bands of the 78-84 post-punk era; *Rip It Up and Start Again*, wrote that - in some respects - *Spiral Scratch* is a more important punk record than the Sex Pistols' *Anarchy in the UK*.

Whereas the Sex Pistols' debut single on EMI demonstrated that *anyone* could step out of the crowd and be in a punk rock band, *Spiral Scratch* proved that anyone could release a record without needing an established record label.

In early 1976 Devoto and Shelley read an NME article that would change everything for the pair. 'Don't look over your shoulder, the Sex Pistols are coming', went the headline. The two students borrowed a car and drove from Manchester to London to see the Pistols live. After the show, they collared Malcolm McLaren and booked the Pistols to play in Manchester at the Lesser Free Trade Hall.

In the audience for that show on the 4th June 1976 are the likes of Morrissey, Mick Hucknall, Ian Curtis, Tony Wilson and Mark E Smith. So that they can play on the same bill as the Pistols when they return to Manchester six weeks later, Howard and Pete form Buzzcocks.

But by early '77 Devoto already wanted to distance himself from the emerging punk scene, which he viewed as quickly becoming a cliché. 'I just don't like movements,' he told the NME later.

'I'm just perverse, like that'.

'Originally, we'd incited people to do something of their own. They were doing something of their own, except it was actually a slavish copy – and a copy of something that hadn't really been there in the first place.'

Then in the summer of 1977, at the height of punk, Devoto pinned up a notice in Manchester's Virgin record store seeking musicians for his heretical new project. 'Punk mentality not essential.'

'*Shot by Both Sides*', Magazine's debut single sounded like an anthem but was the opposite of everything anthems are supposed to be: it was really about *inactivism*. A heroic non-committal.

Devoto symbolically stepping away from the *vulgarity* that he felt typified most of the punk scene.

I wormed my way into the heart of the crowd
I was shocked by what was allowed
I didn't lose myself in the crowd

The lyrics for 'Shot', though, came from a

political argument between *individualist* centrist Devoto and a staunchly left-wing girlfriend. In the end, fed up with Howard's contradictory edict, the girl is said to have declared, 'When they put up the barricades, *you'll end up shot by both sides.*'

That's the convenience of the false dichotomy, it hides nuisance alternatives from consideration. Postmodern culture, of course, is paradoxical by nature and the dissenter is always stuck in between a juxtaposition of opposites. In art, music, literature and advertising, as well as in other media, anything can be juxtaposed to anything else.

A brand or a product can be ridiculed and promoted at the same time and gain advertising *credibility* by advertising that parodies advertising.

On the one hand, this can be creatively liberating, on the other hand it leaves *discerning* planners in a limbo, a state of never being certain which side of the bed they are lying on.

In his autobiography, *Life*, Keith Richards describes how he and Mick initially clicked, in the early days before the Stones happened. He notes that they had almost identical tastes in music (blues, r'n'b) and an almost telepathic understanding, and agreement on which music was right and wrong.

'We'd hear a record and go, That's wrong, That's faking, THAT'S real. It was either that's the shit, or that isn't the shit.
No matter what kind of music you were talking about.
I really liked some pop music. If it was the shit.
But there was a definite line of what the shit was and what wasn't the shit.
Very strict.'

(This level of modernist discernment seems, sadly, kinda quaint in 2019.)

Although, *post*modernity has created the ideal consumers, for sure. We can't get no satisfaction.

And as a postmodern bonus, if everything is *acceptable* and yet *suspect* at the same time, one can simultaneously critique and make fun of oneself for one's consumption behaviour (such as *guilty pleasures*) and still get all the *signalling* benefits of consumer capitalism. The ideal market.

I love the first four or five Billy Joel albums.

Maybe even six. Some people would label Billy a 'guilty pleasure'. I call it discernment. He never became big in the UK really until 'Uptown Girl', but his best stuff predates that. It's *the shit*.

Billy Joel knows a thing or two about what matters.

'As human beings, we need to know that we are not alone, that we are not crazy or completely out of our minds, that there are other people out there who feel as we do, live as we do, love as we do, who are like us.'

There's a great interview Billy did with Alec Baldwin for WNYC radio. The two of them riffing off of each other like a Long Island version of Steve Coogan and Rob Brydon. Of course, Alec Baldwin is occasionally the shit too.

30 rock is one of the funniest things on TV in the last decade or so, and he's responsible for one of the finest 8 minutes cinema history in *Glen Garry Glen Ross* as Blake, the Gary Vee-esque 'motivational' speaker sent in to terrorise a bunch of jaded, underachieving real estate salesmen.

Always. Be. Closing.

(Incidentally, the Blake character was written explicitly for Baldwin in the film version, and is not part of the original play.)

In his review for Time magazine, Richard Corliss said, '... the film is a photo-essay, shot in morgue close-up, about the difficulty most people have convincing themselves that what they do matters'.

It could just as easily have been set in a contemporary ad agency or marketing department.

A bunch of planners trying to convince themselves that what they do, matters.

The bad news is that advertising has always been a weak force.

Because moving human behaviour is difficult.

The new technologies have had the most impact on how we target media spend, but that has not fundamentally changed the role of advertising in how humans make decisions.

Programmatic banners or even 'addressable' TV spots, no matter how data-driven and targeted, are not going to destroy anyone's 'free-will' anytime soon.

Obviously, I'm using 'free-will' as a metaphor here as, strictly speaking, there is no such thing. Paraphrasing Sam Harris, the argument goes that to have free will one would need to be acutely aware of all the factors that determine your thoughts and actions, and you would also need to be able to control these factors. We can't do any of those things.

Yes, we have allowed our Silicon Valley overlords to acquire increased knowledge of our every move. And postmodern business is now hellbent on collecting those vast amounts of data on every aspect of our lives, in the hope of predicting our future behaviour and selling that on to marketers.

But if marketers really did have this 'god-like' power to control consumers behaviour, we'd expect somewhat more impressive CTRs.

The fallacious thinking behind this mythology - although undeniably *paydirt* for charlatans of several flavours and a generous glug of mystification to agency creds decks - was that people can be *programmed just to do, what we want them to.*

For the neo-Marxists and the surveillance-capitalists alike, advertising is the force that brings into existence *wants that previously did not exist.* It supposedly *brainwashes the masses, so they don't notice they are being exploited, alienated from each other.*

If only it were true. The problem with this 'manipulation' view of advertising is that its proponents *and* detractors - despite being ideologically just about as far apart as it is possible to be - both subscribe to the same erroneous beliefs, with the double whammy of each side's misconception reinforcing the other.

And, ironically, as any small increases in understanding of how to influence consumers have been revealed, the channels that worked best for influencing choice have started to become less effective. Delivering a high impact brand experience to a mass of eyeballs on 55inch TV screens would still be the greatest brand-building tactic in the box.

If only those pesky consumers were still watching!

In the end, Magazine did get shot by both sides.

On the fringes of the Top 40, Magazine were invited to appear on Top of the Pops, the weekly British TV chart show. At first, Devoto refused, but the next week, under pressure from their record company, the band agreed to appear. During the 'performance' the alien-like Devoto stood stock-still barely miming the lyrics and freaked out the family audience.

Magazine's small fan base had already bought the record, and the next week it actually went down the charts. This is thought to be the first time in pop history that mass exposure on Top of the Pops made the single go down the charts.

I stole the title for this book from that first Magazine single. In more than twenty years inside the advertising business, *I've wormed my own way into the heart of the crowd* and been *shocked by what was allowed.*

And being stuck inbetween in a false dichotomy is no place to be.

In our business, on one side there is the anti-digital lobby, misty-eyed for the golden age of *unique selling propositions*. On the other are the digital zealots, desperate to declare the death of anything more than 3 weeks old.

You can end up being shot by both sides.

Because you belong to *no* side.

ABOUT THE AUTHOR

After unsuccessful attempts at neo-expressionist painting, pop stardom and, later, Balearic/acid DJ superstardom (although he did achieve one global techno-house hit in the mid-90s) Eaon finally turned to advertising as a last-gasp creative outlet. Initially (and equally unsuccessfully) as a Creative Director he eventually found his calling in Account Planning and Strategy when he found out who Tessa Pollitt's dad was.

To have Eaon come and speak email him at eaonspeaking@gmail.com

BOWIE WAS SHOOTING the video for his big 1980 hit *Ashes to Ashes* on Brighton beach.

Bowie is in full Pagliacci style clown garb, surrounded by Steve Strange and various *Blitz kids*, invited down from London as extras.

In the middle of a scene some old geezer who was out walking his dog, wandered into the shot.

The director totally lost it, and began furiously chasing down the old man.

Bowie said he always remembered this incident any time he got carried away by pop legend notions of self-importance.

Pointing over to Bowie the angry Director berated the grandad.

'Get out of the way!
Don't you know who THIS is?'

'*Yes, I do*', replied the intruder.

'*It's some cunt in a clown suit*'.

Get Eaon's other books

'Where Did It All Go Wrong: Adventures at the Dunning-Kruger Peak of Advertising -' 2017

'Eat Your Greens: Fact based Thinking To Improve Your Brand's Health' - (co-author) 2018

On the run to the outside of everything

Printed in Great Britain
by Amazon

48522437R00156